001376 Ken

I PRAY YOU'LL
GREAT EXPERIEN
THAT GOD WILL RICHLY BLESS
Bruce Rowlison
I Peter 4:9

CREATIVE
HOSPITALITY

As a Means of Evangelism

by Bruce A. Rowlison

Green
Leaf
Press

ISBN 0-938462-03-2

Library of Congress Catalog Card Number 81-84182

Green Leaf Press, P.O. Box 5, Campbell, CA 95009

PRINTED IN THE UNITED STATES OF AMERICA

Contents

Foreword

"Perhaps one of the most important gifts which the Holy Spirit bestows on the believer is the gift of hospitality . . . that genuine expression of Christian love and concern which is so sadly lacking in many areas of our Christian life today. I found Bruce's book CREATIVE HOSPITALITY a very challenging, convincing, and convicting presentation of this unique grace, and I heartily commend it to all."

Cliff Barrows
Program Director
Billy Graham Association

Preface

Creative Hospitality As A Means of Evangelism was born out of a need for following up the visitors who come to a worship service. It is our attempt to follow Paul's example in I Thessalonians 2:8, "So, being affectionately desirous of you, we were ready to share with you not only the gospel of God, but also our own selves, because you had become very dear to us." Many approaches to evangelism stop with the gospel, but hospitality presses us into opening our hearts.

I found in my research in the doctoral program at the Jesuit Theological Seminary at Berkeley that there were many others like me—pastors and laymen —who had excused themselves from evangelism because they weren't extroverts.

Hospitality became a means for a whole new group of people in the church to emerge and exercise their gift. And it is a gift they can use without hours of training classes and lots of pastoral supervision. I am not saying it is easy. It isn't. Hospitality is hard work. But it is practical, and it can motivate a whole new team of people in the church.

Bruce A. Rowlison, D. Min.
Pastor, Gilroy Presbyterian Church
Gilroy, California

Acknowledgements

Excerpts from "A Guide to International Friendship," by Paul E. Little. Used by permission of Inter-Varsity Christian Fellowship.

"I Was Hungry," by Ken Medema, © Copyright 1977 by Word Music, Inc. (A Division of WORD, INC.). All rights Reserved. International Copyright Secured. Used by permission.

Excerpts from *Home Celebrations*, by Lawrence E. Moser. Copyright © 1970 by The Missionary Society of Saint Paul the Apostle in the State of New York. Used by permission of Paulist Press.

Excerpts from *Reaching Out* by Henri J. M. Nouwen. Copyright © 1975 by Henri J. M. Nouwen. Reprinted by permission of Doubleday & Company, Inc.

All scripture quotations are from the Revised Version of the Bible, copyrighted 1946, 1952, © 1971, 1973.

Excerpts from *I Stand by the Door*, by Helen Smith Shoemaker, Word Books. Used by permission.

Excerpts from "Hospitality: Optional or Commanded:" by Edith Schaeffer. Copyrighted 1976 by CHRISTIANITY TODAY. Used by permission.

Introduction

COME! TAKE A TRIP WITH ME.

It is not just another "church party." This one has the element of *surprise*. There is a group of Samoan flame dancers—six of them. They dance. They sing. They tell the story of Hawaiian luaus. There is a real pig rotating on a spit, complete with an apple in its mouth.

This party also has the ingredient of *quality*. There are slides of Hawaii. Long flowered dresses, white pants, and aloha shirts are the early evening dress. Leis are worn by the hostesses. Hawaiian punch and other Hawaiian drinks are served, and, of course, are stirred by sugar cane with Vanda orchids in the drinks and a Japanese parasol sticking out. Special glasses are used. And, floating in the swimming pool, are plants with lit candles in the center.

This party follows the theme so well that it is

an adventure. From the pineapple upside-down cake to the coconut to the exotic salads, the food is a gourmet delight. A photographer is present taking everyone's picture to be mailed to each guest by the host in two weeks with a thank you for coming and bringing some of the food. The relaxing Hawaiian music playing softly in the background adds the final touch to this fun, elegant evening. The Tiki torches stationed appropriately around the yard light your way out.

Even husbands, who only occasionally attend church, go away feeling, "This was a special evening. This evening doesn't fit my childhood experience of Christianity. Maybe there is something more to these people from the church." Said my friend Bill, who hosted the evening, "Every five or ten years I go all out on a party to communicate that Christians can do things well."

Now, let's travel to another party. The same home. A different group. A different approach. Ten professional men came with sleeping bags to share problem cases, journal reviews, etc. The host, Dr. Bill, provided two guest speakers to teach—one on the technical side of their work, and another on the skills of office management. Dinner was catered superbly. Time was scheduled for physical activity: tennis, swimming, sauna, and hot tub.

The list of my friend's unusual parties goes on

and on. How would you like to join in an eight-week Wednesday noon "Poolside Seminar" for busy professional people to drop by and share a brown-bag lunch? You would read appropriate proverbs and discuss such topics as:

—Your marriage and family
—The world of work
—What do you do for exercise?
—What have you learned about finances? Or, you can come join the post-game football party to celebrate the local team's winning season. Then, there is the Jaycees Guest Night Dinner to honor those who have made outstanding community contributions that year. The nearby church Couples' Club is hosted for their Christmas party. Occasionally there is a surprise party to honor one of the staff.

What is the purpose of all this? "Sometimes a lot of bridges have to be built *before* evangelism can take place. Many barriers have to be penetrated before the gospel is heard," said my friend.

I find a great need and a growing desire to take a fresh look at hospitality, and I try to do that in Chapter 2 when we see what hospitality is like. And, in Chapter 6, I brainstorm many different possibilities for hospitality until we find *our style*.

Why is it that in the church we usually violate so many of the rules of hospitality? Where else in our society do we force people to get all dressed up and sit on very hard seats for one hour, and sit in such a position that they can't see anybody's face or be seen by anybody else? We allow them very little movement, though, in recent years, we have been encouraging them to participate more and be less of a spectator. Where else in our society do we ignore so many rules of hospitality? Yet, somehow, we still expect friendliness to happen. In Chapter 5, I have done an in-depth study of obstacles to being hospitable.

Hospitality became a greater option for me when I faced some of my fears and prejudices toward strangers. That was not an easy journey, but it has opened new areas in my personal development. My confidence has increased. My self-image has improved. I have become more assertive and direct in communication with people. I remember sharing with a group of eight friends my struggle to reach out to strangers, and one of them gave me the record, "Nothing Good Comes Easy." Humming that tune has helped make hospitality an adventure, rather than a burden. I have tried to share something of my pilgrimage of converting the stranger into a friend in Chapter 1.

For me, the most valuable part of my study of hospitality was to trace that theme historically and biblically. All the experiments I was doing, all the changes I was experiencing, all the disjointed discoveries I was recording—became unified. Hopefully,

Chapter 4 will do the same for you.

As you reflect on the place hospitality has had in your life, and you boldly experiment in the coming months, I hope you will be able to see great effects from your being hospitable. Then you can finish writing Chapter 7 for me.

This book is intended to be practical, and not just theoretical. Most of the ideas have come from experimenting and studying those who excel in hospitality. This book lends itself to small group discussion. Chapter 8 is a smorgasbord of practical suggestions that I hope you will find helpful.

Converting the Enemy
Into a Guest

I would never accuse the church of being openly hostile to strangers. Open hostility is such an obvious sin that someone might confront us, causing us to become hospitable. The church doesn't elect members like the country club, or give black marbles like service clubs and fraternal organizations. The church is more subtle in its hostility toward visitors. We seat them by themselves in worship. We place Bibles beside us in the pew to save seats for "our friends." We inaugurate a coffee hour to get acquainted with visitors, and then use it to meet our friends. We remember the names of all the people who come into our offices or business during the week, but can't remember the name of the one family we met at church last week.

My own pilgrimage from hostility to hospitality has been arduous and slow.

"Don't ever accept a ride from a stranger!"
"Never go to the bathroom alone at the movies!"
"Don't accept gifts from strangers!"
"Be careful of people you don't know!"
"Watch out for . . . , you just don't know what they might do!"
"Now we had a fellow back home in Nebraska who accepted a ride from . . . and . . ."
It's been thirty years since I received those admonitions and heard those stories, but it seems like yesterday. Helpful they were to a little boy growing up, but now they trouble me when I read biblical injunctions like 1 Peter 4:9, "Practice hospitality ungrudgingly to one another." Yet, the wisdom handed down to me must be true because I have never been beaten up, robbed, raped, embarrassed, or made to look foolish by a stranger, or—so the little voice inside me reasons. And so I keep my distance. In fact, my natural inclination is to request that you have a good list of references, wait a long time, or earn my approval to draw close to me emotionally.

My stance toward the outsider, in spite of biblical commands, has been basically hostile. I own a big German shepherd, leave lights on when I go out, have big locks on all my doors, try to hire someone to live at my home when I go on vacation, deface all my valuables with my driver's license number, place stickers on windows declaring all things are marked, and inform the neighbors to be on the lookout for strangers while I am gone.

I am part of my anxious, suspicious, fearful culture.

For three years I have been doing a number of things in my personal life to move me from hostility to hospitality. I find it very hard work. My natural instinct is to cling to what I own, and to view with suspicion the parts of this world I don't know well. And then, God keeps breaking into my tight, safe structure, and calls me to make the stranger into a guest, my enemy into a friend.

Some historians argue that we are living in the strange era of *Pax Terrora*—the peace of terror. All the powerful nations of the world are aligned in a fearful balance of power. This odd peace is maintained by mutual fear of what might happen should all weapons be unleashed. Years ago, there was the *Pax Romana*—peace of Rome. The powerful, totalitarian Roman government made it possible to live and travel in peace. Then there was the *Pax Brittania*—peace of Great Britain. The great British Empire brought a sense of order and peace to the whole world. So, now, these historians argue, we are experiencing a world peace resulting from fear. The ones who will have the most effective ministry will be the people who learn how to live in the age of fear so characterized by anxiety, apathy, and violence. Our temptation is to pull in, rather than reach out. Our natural inclination is to strengthen our family, our clan, our race, our church, and protect ourselves against "them." Again, the gospel breaks into our retreats and calls us to advance and make the stranger into a guest.

Who is the stranger?

Who is the stranger toward whom I have a love-hate relationship?

The stranger is not just the person I've never met before or gotten to know. It can be the beautiful, recent divorcee I've known for a long time who now suddenly threatens my marriage by her presence. It is my friend who has suffered a double tragedy which I can't handle, so I have pushed him to the periphery of my life. It is my friend who changes his values and life style and, suddenly, I find myself avoiding him entirely. I can't handle his differentness. The stranger for me is the one who expresses his anger in a way with which I cannot cope. It is my quiet friend who nods and smiles at my stories, but never lets me really know what he is thinking. The stranger is the one who comes and grabs me, and hugs me, and demands more affection than I can give at that moment. I retreat into my shell. At other times, the stranger is the one whose pilgrimage of faith and theology is different from mine.

Sometimes, for me, the stranger to whom the quiet voice of God's Spirit whispers—"reach out"—is my friend—the enemy!

A little boy came home from his first day at Sunday School and his mother asked him how he liked it. The child replied, "I hated it. They put me in a room full of children all by myself." That is the same feeling of many adults when they attend worship. The church is often a lonely crowd.

How many times on vacation have you visited a church and learned how lonely it is when the service is over and no one bothers to greet or speak to you, the visitor? At times like that you feel something of the Psalmist's sad words, "No one cares for me." Many questions rattle through your mind. If you aren't welcome in the Lord's house, where are you welcome? Does this happen often in the church where you belong? Who is responsible to see that visitors are made to feel at home? How can we get our members to express friendship to newcomers and make them welcome? Is it the responsibility of each one of us to see that our church is a friendly church? Would you be willing to reach out to a visitor? What does the Bible say about friendship? hospitality? caring?

I took a course on "Grief," and the professor assigned us the task of interviewing persons who had experienced loss within the past two years: a person who had lost a loved one; another who had suffered loss in divorce; and one who experienced loss through moving. After the interviews, we were to write a one-page summary of each one and present it to the class. The startling discovery for me was that the grief process was the same in each instance. I asked them to describe their grief, what they felt, where they turned for help, what help was received, and what help was needed and not received.

The people's need to receive hospitality was incredible. They talked about anger, hurt, acute loneliness, difficulty reaching out, unhappiness, fatigue. They pictured being exploded and not quite able to gather all their parts and be made whole. They described being in the bottom of a cold well, alone. They said they felt like they were in a tunnel unable to see any light at either end. They told of the tension of needing to be alone, yet desiring to be with a few friends. The professor had me read these feelings to the class, and they were to guess death, divorce, or moving. The class unanimously thought death. Wrong! Those were the feelings of people who moved from one city to another, or went through divorce. The need for someone to reach out to them was enormous.

I had always thought crisis is what brought people *to* the church. Now I am discovering crisis, without loving care and support and interest of the church, is what motivates people to *leave* the church for cults and any other substitute they can find. The time to practice loving hospitality is now.

If ever an era needed hospitality, it is ours. People are love starved. Our technological society is turning some people into "Star Wars" robots. The nuclear family is disintegrating. Marriages are becoming so fragile that they can't bear the pressure of one child without falling apart. Romantic love is becoming bankrupt, and we are seeing the rise of arranged marriages—especially in some cults. The authority structure in the family, school, business, and much of society is in disarray. People are so desperate for love they will sacrifice their intellectual integrity and join bizarre groups which reach out to them. If there were ever a need for Christians to practice hospitality, it is now.

Many people in and out of our churches are so hungry for love that they will settle for electronic friendship—the Christian television program. At least they can call a number and give someone a prayer request. Or, they can call and someone will listen to them. Or, they can call and give money. And they do —by the thousands. Somehow, it seems we in the church have such a secure, happy fellowship that we can't comprehend the life of the majority of the people being wounded or crushed by our impersonal society.

QUESTIONS FOR REVIEW AND DISCUSSION:

1. How have you been welcomed in churches?

2. How do I reach out to new people in the church?
    What is my *modus operandi*?
    How am I most comfortable extending myself?

3. Who is the stranger toward whom I have a love-hate relationship?
    Are there any individuals or groups of people who bring fear to my heart?

4. Can you think of the names of two new people you have met in the last month at your church?

5. As you think of the visitors who attend your church, and those new people who move into your apartment or community, what feelings begin to emerge? Write them down.

❧ 2 ❧

Hospitality Is Like

WHAT IS HOSPITALITY LIKE?
- —an open door where they take you in
- —a place where you are listened to and not "put down"
- —a hospice where there is shelter
- —the holy of holies where the presence of Christ is shared
- —a couch where "reality checks" take place
- —a party where people celebrate
- —a hospital where healing takes place
- —a home where you can be yourself
- —a cozy ski lodge where friendships are made
- —a bench at the park where you can reflect and reminisce
- —a sanctuary where the sacrament of communion happens
- —a camp where you are cared for, and people give themselves to you

> —a little nook where you can live without fear,
> and experience community

WHAT HOSPITALITY IS *NOT* NECESSARILY LIKE . . .

Words easily lose their deepest meanings and, thus, their strengths. One example is the word "fellowship." Christians tend to consider every encounter as fellowship even when it is destructive or superficial. Hospitality has suffered from a similar misuse. Sweet, plastic smiles, back-slapping, safe conversations, and comfortableness are not necessarily synonomous with hospitality.

Henri Nouwen, in his book *Reaching Out* describes what hospitality is like by tracing the meaning of the word in different languages.

> In the German, the word for hospitality
> is *Gastfreundschaft* which means "the free-
> dom of the guest."[1]

Nouwen talks about the relationship of freedom to hospitality. He argues that hospitality is creating a free and friendly space for people. I agree that part of hosting is to allow the guest room or space for God to do as he pleases in his life. And I agree that it is one of the most difficult tasks to do. When people with different backgrounds, values, and goals get close to me, they touch many of my insecurities in a very short time. To give them space and freedom is hard work.

Hospitality is opening our lives to people. It is a way of ministering to an impersonal, lonely, fast-moving, fearful, technological society. The old reformer John Calvin once prayed, "O God . . . My heart I give Thee, eagerly and sincerely." That is the way it is with hospitality. We open our hearts to God and as we do so, we open our hearts to our brother. We become willing to take risks, be inconvenienced, and give of ourselves.

A number of theological questions are tied together. Who is God? Who is my neighbor? Am I my brother's keeper? The scriptures refuse to let these questions be separated. It is not possible to love God and hate (ignore) our brother, declares John the apostle.[2]

Hospitality is developing the *attitude of a servant*. In John 13, Jesus puts on "the apron" and serves the disciples. It was not beneath his dignity to take the basin and towel, get down on his knees, and dirty his hands to serve others. John Stott, reflecting on how Jesus reached out to serve people, told this story.

In 1878 when William Booth's Salvation Army had just been so named, men from all over the world began to enlist. One man,

who had once dreamed of himself as a
bishop, crossed the Atlantic from America
to England to enlist. He was a Methodist
minister, Samuel Logan Brengle. And he
now turned from a fine pastorate to join
Booth's Salvation Army. Brengle later
became the Army's first American-born
Commissioner. But at first Booth accepted
his services reluctantly and grudgingly.
Booth said to Brengle, "You've been your
own boss too long." And in order to instill
humility into Brengle, he set him to work
cleaning the boots of other trainees. And
Brengle said to himself, "Have I followed
my own fancy across the Atlantic in order
to black boots?" Then, as in a vision, he
saw Jesus bending over the feet of rough,
unlettered fishermen. "Lord," he whis-
pered, "You washed their feet; I will black
their boots."[3]

So, is the Lord calling us to allow our floors to
get dirty and our furniture worn and dishes broken
in our obedience to host people for his glory? It is
obvious that hospitality is more than just throwing a
party. Sometimes it means weeping with a friend, or
staying up late listening to his story. It is not simply
a quick prayer for someone, but, like old Abraham,

we may be called on to share our tent, food, family, friends.

My parents had the privilege to be served by about fifteen pastors in their lives. The pastor who stands above all others is the one who served them best. My father suffered a serious heart attack and spent a long time in the hospital. The pastor and his wife cared for my family by babysitting, shoveling the snow-filled sidewalk, and grocery shopping. Thirty-five years later that minister is remembered with affection and appreciation above all others. That is what hospitality is like.

Hospitality is like a hospice on a lonely journey. Have you seen and heard the true story of Alfredo? Teleketics Films shows the story of a destitute boy in Mexico. When he was very young, Alfredo's home was burned. All his family was killed in the fire and he was left with scars he could not hide, homeless, and a beggar. One day he heard children laughing and playing and singing in the "Hacienda," an orphanage. He sought out the "father" of these children and begged to join this extended family. The padre had the other children make the decision on whether to receive Alfredo, to assure acceptance by everyone. It was a moving moment when this badly scarred and lonely boy stood before the whole group. Suddenly a boy reached out and took his hand, *"Tu eres mi hermano"* (you are my brother), and all the children welcomed him with music and fireworks and dancing. Which of us has not needed the place of acceptance along our journey? Hospitality is providing that place of warmth and acceptance.

QUESTIONS FOR REVIEW AND DISCUSSION:

1. Finish this statement: Hospitality is like . . .

2. The people who have demonstrated hospitality to me are . . .

3. The things that these people have done which have communicated hospitality are . . .

4. Can you describe a time when you felt rejected by God's people?

5. Do you agree with Henri Nouwen that hospitality is creating free and friendly space for people?

6. As you picture Jesus bending over the feet of rough, unlettered fishermen, do you see the faces of any persons he is asking you to serve ungrudgingly?

3

Models of Hospitality

GOD AS THE GRACIOUS HOST

When we look for models of hospitality, a great place to begin is with God, himself. The Psalmist, in Psalm 23, describes God as a gracious host who extends generous hospitality to me and treats me as his royal guest. Look at the *details* the host tends to. God has spread a table before me to eat until I am full. He is protecting me against my enemies, physically and emotionally. He provides refreshing and cleansing with oils. He is quenching my thirst with a cup of water or wine so full that some of it spills as I bring it to my thirsty lips.

So, how do we take the qualities of a perfect host in the ancient Middle East and apply them to our community? What are the most pressing needs of the new people in our community?

—a list of suggested babysitters

    —an invitation to dinner

    —a simple cup of coffee together

    —someone who listens to them

    —acceptance by a new community which doesn't come through the Chamber of Commerce brochure

In Hawaii, hospitality includes a floral lei. In England, one receives an early morning cup of tea and a roll. In Japan, your host bows to you, and polishes your shoes left outside the door. What will hospitality be like in your city and mine?

THE GOOD SAMARITAN'S MODEL OF HOSPITALITY

Jesus gave significant models of hospitality through his teaching. In Luke 10, when Jesus answers questions of how to receive eternal life and "who is my neighbor?" he takes them on a guided visualization of loving hospitality. We see reflections of Psalm 23, where God graciously hosts us to a festive banquet. Here, Jesus portrays the Samaritan disrupting his schedule to carefully treat the wounds and take the injured man to the inn, and see that he is restored to full health. It was a beautiful twist to have the questioner's enemy be the hospitable one.

REACHING OUT TO THE HANDICAPPED

In Luke 14, Jesus taught that true hospitality

was extended as an act of mercy, not for personal reward or promotion. So he challenged us to invite the poor, crippled, lame, blind to our parties—not our friends, relatives, and the influential people around us. Someone has said that our check stubs gossip about our priorities. I think the same could be said about our list of party invitations. What feast will we soon be preparing for the overlooked people in our community?

MARY AND MARTHA AS A HOSPITABLE TEAM

Mary and Martha combined to provide significant, satisfying hospitality. Jesus had a deep friendship with Lazarus, but I am sure he went to Bethany many times because of the welcome of Mary and Martha. We tend to focus on the single instance of their quarrel each time we study them, but much could be said about their teamwork. Martha was seeing to the details of food and house decor, while Mary was giving herself to guests. I am sure that not only the Savior felt comfortable there, but a lot of other people as well. Jesus returned to their home on a number of occasions, and was refreshed.

JAPANESE TEA CEREMONY

If we look outside the scriptures, *for present day models of hospitality*, one of the first places I would direct your attention to is the Japanese Tea

Ceremony. Some years ago, I spent two months in Japan living with eleven different families. I experienced the Tea Ceremony at least 30 times. The feelings I put in my diary were, "restful, serene, privileged, humbled, welcomed, honored."

The ceremony has a fixed form and dates back to the sixteenth century. You have a host and a very small group, enabling intimacy. The movement in the preparation and distribution is carefully prescribed. The visitor is honored in many special ways. The environment is thoroughly cleaned, utensils carefully selected, fire kindled, the room decorated with a natural beauty, plus a flower arrangement in the *tokonoma*, and a piece of artistry, such as a scroll, painting, or porcelain vase, appropriate to the occasion. Yet the room is so simple, the focus remains on the people. There is privacy. There is quiet. There is reflection and dialogue. You often walk through a garden to get to the tiny Tea House, and during the ceremony everyone sits with a clear view of the garden. I was bowed to, smiled at, and attended to with the greatest of care—real Eastern hospitality.

L'ABRI FELLOWSHIP IN SWITZERLAND

Another illustration of hospitality is the L'Abri Fellowship in Switzerland. Much has been said about the lectures of Francis Schaeffer. Often overlooked is the behind-the-scenes hospitality of Edith Schaeffer.

Here is an example of her demonstration of that gift.

Which shall I do first, go upstairs and write that article that is due, or go out to the garden and pick lettuce and some roses before the frost spoils them? I hesitated, wishing I could go both directions at once. Just then the doorbell rang, and I chose a third direction, the steps down to the front door. "I'm sorry to bother you, but this is an emergency. Can we talk to you now?" My husband was talking to someone in the living room, so I led mother and daughter into the dining room to listen to the problem.

Weeping with those who weep takes time. Two hours later when my husband had come in to join us, I glanced at the clock and realized that everyone needed some food. Slipping out, I put together the ingredients for an eggnog milk shake and started it whizzing, then dipped out broth from bones on the stove and added chicken bouillon and chopped parsley to give more flavor, then cut pieces of homemade brown bread and topped them with cheese and bacon and tomato slices and slipped them into the oven. A nutritious meal was soon

ready for me to carry in on individual
trays, without breaking into the flow of the
conversation. Not only was the food
needed for energy by each of us, but the
pleasantness was remembered afterwards,
and the beauty of a simple meal treasured,
even by someone whose mind was filled
with recent disaster and whose eyes were
blurred with tears.[1]

My friends who visited L'Abri said that much of
the biblical teaching and interaction was made effective by Mrs. Schaeffer's loving, sensitive sacrifice. She
was modeling the Christian love Francis was teaching
in the scriptures. It was her example that made the
scripture come alive. Some people reported, "She
made the gospel believable."[2] Students flocked to
L'Abri to discover truth and experience agape love.

THE TEACHER
Who of us cannot point to a teacher who has
been able to make each student feel special by a
gentle word of appreciation, a note of encouragement
on a paper, or a touch expressing non-verbal affirmation? For me it was an athletic coach who took a
special interest in me during the emotionally turbu-
lent, roller coaster, Junior High years. It was the skills
he taught me which helped me to excel and balance

my low self image. His nurturing of my athletic ability also led to athletic success which contributed to the approval of the student body and the establishment of important friendships. For another it may be the drama coach who demanded the perfections that resulted in excellence which built self confidence. Many people have chosen professions today because of the marvelous impact one teacher had on their lives years ago.

OUR CHILDREN'S FRIENDS

Karen Mains, in her book, *Open Heart, Open Home*, has a chapter entitled "Telltale Marks," where she describes great opportunities for ministry by just being hospitable to her children's friends. She describes the footprints, fingerprints, scattered toys, and high-pitched voices that are a part of the friendships. But the candid comments by the neighbor children make it all worthwhile. We have the privilege of treating children with a respect and dignity they may never have gotten at home. We have the chance to introduce them to such biblical concepts as: children are very precious to God; people are more important than things; each person is created in God's image.

PARENTS'   RELATIONSHIPS   WITH   THEIR CHILDREN

In his book, *Reaching Out*, Henri Nouwen also

views the relationship between parents and children in terms of hospitality. His focus is on the Bible's teaching that children are a precious gift from God to be loved and cared for, not something we own and rule and dominate. Children are like strangers coming into our lives, with their own uniqueness of style, rhythm, and idiosyncrasies. It requires time, patience, and energy to make them feel at home. Thus, the scriptures call us to give to our children what every stranger needs—acceptance, love, time, safety, friendship, space, and freedom.[3] One of the most powerful posters I have ever seen had the picture of a child and the caption, "A child is someone who comes into your life for a brief time and then disappears into an adult."

CROSSING THE GENERATION BARRIER

In the age of mobility in which we live we have found ourselves with a transient church. The concept of church family, which former generations enjoyed, now takes a massive amount of time and energy to create. Children grow up hundreds of miles from grandparents. Specialization in church ministry tends to segregate the ages. One of my friends has made it a point to have people of all ages in their home for Thanksgiving and Christmas dinners—unclaimed widows or widowers, married couples, young singles, and children. It is amazing what some singing, sharing,

parlor games (like Monopoly and Sorry) can do to
enable one generation to touch another.

THE IONA ABBEY

The famous Iona Abbey is built on the site of
the first Christian community in Scotland, founded
by St. Columba in 563 A.D. The folk at the Abbey
take hospitality so seriously that they appoint a
"Guestmaster" whose duties include extending hospitality to all visitors. In recent years scores of tourists
and pilgrims have been warmly received. These Christians take Peter's exhortation seriously: "Practice
hospitality ungrudgingly to one another." (I Peter 4:9)

GARDEN GROVE COMMUNITY CHURCH—LAY MINISTERS OF HOSPITALITY

Since the church's inception in 1955, Dr. Robert
Schuller has emphasized cordially receiving guests and
visitors to the worship service and the surrounding
campus (as they call their church grounds). The
church has carefully and meticulously trained hundreds of Lay Ministers of Hospitality. These people
serve as instant welcoming committees and mini information centers. Their task is to give people a
glorious welcome, and they do it in the name of
Christ.

FROM THE PULPIT TO THE PANTRY

While teaching a course in liturgics, the Rev. Jeff Smith, former chaplain of the Univeristy of Puget Sound, was captivated by the concept of the table in the history of worship. The next semester he taught a class entitled "Food As Sacrament and Celebration." Smith traced the centrality of the table in ancient Israel as well as the church today. Israel was required to feed the stranger and even their enemies. He discovered, however, that they did not have to sit at the table with them. In the church today the communion table is central to worship whether it is called the Eucharist or the Lord's Supper.

Smith's language research resulted in the discovery that there was no Hebrew word for "community" so they began to use the table and eating together as the symbol to convey that idea. Every religious gathering in ancient Israel included food.

Well, the end of the story goes like this. When the University administration required Jeff Smith to get a Ph.D. in theology, he opened a restaurant and cookshop in Tacoma, Washington, called the Chaplain's Pantry. That led to a television show and two Emmy nominations. In addition to cooking for people, his ministry includes periodically greeting people, finding them seats, and ministering to their needs. The Rev. Jeff Smith has taken his ministry from the pulpit to the pantry.[4]

CREATIVE ENTERTAINING AND CELEBRATION

Santa Clara County in California has discovered that one way to cope with the increasing alcohol abuse problem is to train people to be better hosts and hostesses. They have compiled bookets entitled "Creative Entertaining," teaching people how to help their friends socialize without undue dependence on alcohol. They have a staff of four people who go to churches and community groups discussing the problem and presenting solutions. They approach creative entertaining as a means to prevent alcoholism.

I have an underlying conviction that many people, Christians included, expect the *church* to teach one how to worship and the *world* to teach one how to celebrate, and never the two shall meet. The church teaches us how to pray and study the Bible and observe communion and baptism and sing religious songs. But what does the church know about retirement dinners, election victory parties, athletic conquests, and the use of leisure? How do we celebrate the end of a hard day at work? passing the advancement exam? getting the job promotion? another anniversary or birthday? a child's graduation? Television advertisement teaches us "you only go around once in life, so you should grab all the gusto you can," or, "if it is a really special event—serve Lowenbrau."

One of the great things the church could teach
our culture is *how* to celebrate. Not all of the Old
Testament Hebrew religious events were somber,
pious occasions. Many of their religious events were
holy celebrations and festivals, complete with holy
dances and spiritual feasts.

I am sure that some of my friends who know the
Bible best and have an intimate, personal, meaningful
relationship with Christ, would be tremendously
more effective in evangelism if they weren't so awk-
ward socially. Somehow they rarely find a common
ground with non-Christians or nominal Christians.
Some churches and Christian groups feed this sad
problem by getting people involved in as many Bible
studies as possible, and extend them as long as possible, and make such imbalance a badge of spiritual
maturity. How well I remember the week-long camp
of high schoolers which had Bible Study from
9:30 a.m. to 12:15 p.m., and seminars from 2:00 p.m.
to 3:00 p.m., and from 3:30 p.m. to 4:30 p.m. After
dinner they met again from 7:30 p.m. to 9:30 p.m.
for Bible messages. That kind of stuffing disregards
wholeness in life. I get the feeling that many Christians feel Jesus should have used the whip at the
marriage feast in Cana in Galilee and performed the
miracle of turning the water into wine at the temple
in Jerusalem. Our Lord did not hold himself aloof
from human happiness. Those who are his followers

should never forget that.

If our parties are boring people, we certainly are not advancing the gospel. If our parties are embarrassing people, we aren't advancing the kingdom of right relationships. If people are being left out and encouraged to be wall flowers, we need to rethink what we are doing. The church should stimulate its members to evaluate its activities in the light of good hospitality. We need to rethink the biblical concept of celebration, and develop more creative approaches to it.

What models of hospitality would you add to the examples I have given? Is there a neighbor, physician, teacher, psychologist, or social worker who stands out in your mind, who has so touched your life with loving service that it affects the way you treat strangers?

QUESTIONS FOR REVIEW AND DISCUSSION:

1. As you reflect on hospitality customs around the world, what are some of the unique hospitality customs of your own area?

2. When was the last time you did something special for a handicapped person? Plan something special with such a person in the next 30 days.

3. Can you remember when your needs were attended to in an outstanding way?

4. What kinds of conflict do you experience to be hospitable to the person calling on the phone or knocking at the door when you desire to
    —finish the book you are reading?
    —complete the project half done?
    —see the TV football game now in the fourth quarter?

5. What are some other great biblical insights that you can communicate to your children and their friends by just being hospitable?

❧ 4 ❧

Hospitality As a
Biblical Concept

Why should we risk reaching out to strangers?
Why not regroup with the core in our churches until
our foundation is stronger? We need to look at some
scriptural teaching on this topic.

The basic reason we practice hospitality is that
it is an expression of love. The Greek word for hospitality is *philoxenos* which means "lover of strangers."
You can see that hospitality has the same root as the
word "philadelphia" which means "brotherly love."
So, when we exercise hospitality, we are expressing
love for another person.

A number of scripture passages reinforce the
word study. Galatians 6:2 commands us to bear one
another's burdens. In 3 John 5 we read: "Beloved,
it is a loyal thing you do when you render any service to the brethren, *especially to strangers* . . . ."
One practical way we bear burdens includes hospital-

ity, and that is a definite expression of love. Love is meant to be expressed in acts, not just in warm feelings. Hospitality is one way to take love out of the realm of theory and make it a part of our daily lives.

HOSPITALITY AS A GOD-GIVEN GIFT

The New Testament gives at least four specific motives for practicing hospitality. First is because God has gifted us in that area. Peter writes, "Practice hospitality ungrudgingly to one another. As each has received a gift, employ it for one another as good stewards of God's varied grace." (I Peter 4:9,10)

What *is* the gift of hospitality? It is the opening of your home, or hosting guests or strangers generously, joyously, without a lot of complaining. It is opening your life to another person. As an associate pastor, Ron had a great ability to listen and share his life with people. Seminarians would press him, "What is your program? Where are your goals? Where are you going in life? When are you going to get a church of your own?" He replied, "About 30% of my ministry is spent 'covering the door' or caring for people everybody else is too programmed to help." With some he had coffee, with others he walked around the block a couple of times, a few he took home for lunch. When he left after eight years, the church was unable to replace him.

Or, there was Judy, the housewife everyone seemed to go to in their hour of need. So many people called her on the phone that her husband got her a long extension cord, making it possible for her to cook dinner, wash dishes, or tidy up the house while listening to people and caring for them. Somehow, more and more people had that inner knowledge that Judy cared. She listened without judging. She affirmed them. And she knew when to speak a strong word. We three pastors knew she had as great a pastoral ministry as any of us. Hospitality is a God-given gift to be used in ministry to the body of Christ and strangers. Its exercise results in so blessing people that it produces maturity and unity.

How can you recognize the gift of hospitality in a church? One good way is to determine at whose home the youth like to congregate. Another is to listen for the gut-level reactions of adults. I can remember walking out of an exceptionally good church Christmas party in a church officer's home. The food, decorations, mood, and content of the party were beautifully orchestrated. Walking to my car, another guest approached me and said, "You know, Charlie is brilliant, creative, and eloquent, but I don't feel he loves me. I felt manipulated tonight." I stood frozen with my jaw dropped, my keys dangling from my hand, as the man got in his car and drove away. Adults can feel an underlying resentment, tolerance, endurance, vs. a generous welcome. Even the fancy meal with pomp and splendor cannot cover up the underlying attitude of the host and hostess. And, in the scriptures, hospitality is an attitude toward other people—sometimes in your clan—but primarily the outsider, the stranger, the visitor. Are people blessed? Are their hearts warmed? Have their needs been served? Are they made to feel special? Are they genuinely welcomed?

It is amazing to me how the church has a tendency to bury the gift of hospitality. Some of our churches parade the more mysterious gifts of tongues, healing, working of miracles, and prophecy. Other churches encourage and give strokes for the traditional gifts of preaching, teaching, wisdom, knowledge, and administration. My experience has been that when you begin to affirm the gift of hospitality in people they are surprised. They give you that stunned look. When I said to the one who organizes, recruits, trains, and oversees our Sunday School, "You seem to have the gift of administration," he replied a quick, "Thank you." When I said to Jim, "It appears that God has gifted you as a teacher and I want to encourage you to continue developing that gift," he smiled from ear to ear and there was a twinkle in his eye, and he nodded his head with great appreciation.

On the other hand, I said to Mrs. Larson, after a beautiful party in her home, "Standing here at the door and listening to people tell you how they felt welcomed, appreciated, honored, refreshed, and that this is the best time they've had in weeks, means you are a very gifted hostess. God says a lot of good things about hospitality, and I want to affirm your gift." She began an incredible denial system. "Oh, I don't have that gift! Anybody could do what I did. It was nothing." There was no smile. She was embarrassed. She shrugged her shoulders. She almost hung her head in apology. When Mrs. Larson's response was multiplied a half dozen times, it finally dawned on me that in most cases the church has never affirmed the gift of hospitality in its members. Yet, some persons have beautifully developed that gift with very little encouragement. Therefore, when they are appreciated in any way other than "bring those girls out of the kitchen so we can give them a round of applause," they have a hard time believing us. We need to find ways of affirming the gift of hospitality besides putting the person in charge of the big church pot-luck dinner.

In summary, we practice hospitality because God has gifted many of us in that area. And he has strongly urged us to develop and use that gift.

HOSPITALITY HAS A FUTURE
ACCOUNTABILITY

There is also an end-time accountability reason for practicing hospitality. All peoples are part of a natural brotherhood of which the apostle Paul says that God "made from one every nation of men to live on all the face of the earth" (Acts 17:26). Even the ancient Greeks extended hospitality to strangers religiously because of the fear of the gods judging them harshly, and because of a love for their fellow men.

In the Old Testament, God increases Israel's basis for hospitality. In addition to the common brotherhood of man, Israel had another reason for treating the stranger and foreigner kindly. It is a logical and deeply emotional reason. If we take a little journey (in our mind's eye), it might help us feel the impact of God's command. For 400 years you were strangers living in Egypt as slaves. You were ignored, unwelcomed, left out, embarrassed, uncomfortable. You paid your dues, but you felt like you never belonged—and you didn't. You were not accepted. Therefore, in Leviticus 19:18, God commands the children of Israel, "Do not take revenge on anyone or continue to hate him, but love your neighbor as you love yourself." And again, in Leviticus 19:33-34, "Do not mistreat foreigners who are living in your land. Treat them as you would a fellow Israelite, and love them as you would yourselves. Remember that you were once foreigners in the land of Egypt." Israel was to show hospitality to strangers because they know painfully well what it is like to be a foreigner.

In Deuteronomy 10:18,19, the demands of God
are made clear: "He executes justice for the fatherless
and the widow, and loves the sojourner, giving him
food and clothing. Love the sojourner therefore; for
you were sojourners in the land of Egypt." So, show-
ing hospitality is not so much a matter of feeling hospitable as in obeying what God commands.

Jesus built on this theme of accountability for
our hospitality in Matthew 25. "How did you treat
the stranger?" is a judgment question related to our
eternal destiny. What stronger basis do we need to
take hospitality seriously? Jesus talks about feeding
and giving drink to the stranger; receiving him into
our home; clothing, visiting and caring for him. Then
he stuns us by saying he is the stranger.

In Matthew 10, Jesus taught the apostles
embarking on their first mission that the homes
which opened to them would be blessed, and the vil-
lages and towns and homes that did not welcome
them would be cursed.

The apostle Paul links the Gentiles' basis for
hospitality with Israel. To the Romans, Paul says
about the Gentiles that they were outside God's
family and foreigners and strangers until the present
day. Therefore, the Gentiles should treat the outsider
graciously. So, we *all* stand under the command of
God to deal mercifully with the stranger! We were all

strangers once. Therefore, we ought to show special mercy to the stranger. In addition, we will face an accounting before God one day on how we treated the stranger. Some of us have the gift of hospitality, but all of us stand before God with a responsibility to the outsider.

HOSPITALITY INVOLVES AN ENCOUNTER WITH GOD

Then there is a beyond-the-comprehensible reason for practicing hospitality. Scripture bears witness to the abstract reality of angelic visitations. In Genesis 19, two angels came to Lot as ordinary men, warning him of the impending disaster. The patriarch Abraham, as he rested at the door of his tent by the sacred oaks of Mamre, in the hottest part of the day, saw three men approaching and invited them to stop and refresh themselves. In the best of Eastern hospitality, he bowed to them and offered to serve them in specific ways. He offered them shade beneath the tree and water to wash their feet, and cakes of meal and curds and milk, and a freshly butchered calf. It turned out that one of the three was either the Lord himself or his angel (Genesis 18:1-8,22).

The writer of the Hebrews urges us: "Remember to welcome strangers in your homes. There were some who did that and welcomed angels without knowing it" (Hebrews 13:2). The warning is that there just may be real angelic visitations again. Don't throw away this possible good fortune.

In Matthew 25, Jesus repeats this idea when he calls himself the stranger who visits us. Again, in Matthew 10:40, he compares the welcoming of strangers to the welcoming of God.

HOSPITALITY HAS MISSIONARY POSSIBILITIES

Finally, we practice hospitality because of its missionary possibilities. Not only may you entertain angels unaware, but you may welcome many into the household of God. The New Testament demonstrates again and again that hospitality serves the gospel.

Much of *Jesus' ministry* depended on hospitality that people extended to him. In Mark 1:29 and following, Jesus is in Peter's home and heals his mother-in-law. In the evening, the neighbors feel comfortable enough to bring people sick with all kinds of diseases for Jesus to heal. In Mark 2:1-12, Jesus does his teaching in a home in Capernaum. Later, Levi throws a party for all his tax collecting buddies which affords Jesus entre into another segment of society. At the home of Jairus, in Mark 5, Jesus confronted death and the professional mourners and the despair of the family. In Mark 15, while Jesus is at the house of Simon, Mary annoints him for his coming burial, resulting in some powerful interaction with the other guests. In Mark 15, Jesus uses the intimacy of the upper room of a home to prepare his disciples for his way to the cross. Hospitality was crucial to Jesus' ministry. It propelled the gospel forward into people's lives.

Not only Jesus' ministry was very much built upon hospitality, but when our Lord first sent out the disciples, he counted on hospitality. In Matthew 10 and Luke 10, Jesus sends the apostles to homes, and they are dependent upon a welcome. "Bless the homes that receive you, and pronounce a judgment on the homes that turn you away."

Even the early church continued the pattern of Jesus and his apostles. In Acts 10, the Gentile Cornelius is richly blessed by the hospitality he afforded Simon Peter. In Acts 16, Lydia from Thyatira was living in Philippi and opened her home to Paul and Silas and Timothy. Her hospitality proved to be a center for the thrust of the gospel in that area. In Acts 17, the gospel penetrates the community because Jason opened his home to the disciples. In Acts 18, the gospel gets firmly established in Corinth because Aquila and Priscilla receive Paul in their home for an extended period of time.

Just as hospitality served to advance the gospel in Jesus' ministry and the disciples' work, so today it can be one of our richest means of missionary activity. International Students Incorporated can never find enough Christian homes in which to place students

from other countries. The American Field Service and
the Rotary Exchange programs are additional opportunities to exercise this gift. James Kennedy of the
Coral Ridge Presbyterian Church, and author of
Evangelism Explosion, said humorously that they
have so trained their lay people in evangelism and
home hospitality that, when the Mormons and Jeho-
vah's Witnesses come to their doors, they lock the
door—*after* they let them in.[1]

Think of how many missionaries caught the
vision for world mission as young children when their
parents had various missionaries stay in their home
for a few days. Impressions made in those early for-
mative years yielded rich fruit years later.

We ask the participants in each membership
class what it is that drew them to our church. I wish
I could say it was the theology of the church, or great
sermons, or a terrific youth program, but the over-
whelming initial response is "the friendship of the
people." And when I visit newcomers who haven't
returned to worship with us, their frequent response
is, "We came to the coffee hour between services and
nobody spoke to us." Last Sunday we had a well-
known guest speaker in our worship service, and he
told me at lunch that he had worshiped four years in
a church as a widower and only two families ever had
him to a dinner—and the one family was cousin to his
late wife, and the other was his bishop. Isn't it time

we begin to reemphasize the biblical mandate to be hospitable as integral to the fulfillment of the Great Commission?

I believe the passage of scripture that has drawn more people to the Lord in this generation than any other Bible verse is Revelation 3:20. Jesus says, "Behold, I stand at the door and knock; if any one hears my voice and opens the door, I will come in to him and eat with him, and he with me." I have always heard that verse explained in terms of hospitality. The door is the door of our lives. Jesus wants to come into our lives and have a relationship with us. In the Middle East, during the first century, people didn't have hotels and motels along the travel routes, so they were dependent upon people opening their homes. And when you took a stranger in, you fed him, got acquainted with him, and gave him a place to stay. You had fellowship with him. Now, God comes to you in Jesus Christ and knocks on the door of your life, desiring fellowship with you. He never forces his way in. He lets you open the door.

As a host or hostess you have at least three alternatives. You can ignore the knock and hope that he will go away. You can open the door and tell him to go away. You can open the door and invite him in and share your life with him. And you can invite him into your life by prayer which is a conversation with God.

> Lord Jesus, I now open the door of my
> life and receive you as my Savior and
> Lord. Thank you for coming into my
> life.

Of course, the content of the gospel precedes this
ritual: The acknowledgement of who God is, the human predicament of sin and separation, our inability
to resolve our human predicament, our desire to repent (turn about) and submit to Jesus' leadership in
our lives. The receiving of Jesus into our life as an
initial step seems to be universally understood
through the vehicle of hospitality.

QUESTIONS FOR REVIEW AND DISCUSSION:

1. Describe your hospitality toward God.
    Is God the stranger in your life?
    Have you invited him into your life and made
    peace and friendship with him?

2. Has God given you the gift of hospitality?

3. Whom do you know that has that gift?

4. How have you affirmed people with that gift?

Barriers to
Reaching Out

THE PASTOR'S TRAINING

One obstacle in reaching out to new people is that many pastors are introverted and have learned in seminary how to hide from people. Pastors have been taught how to analyze Bible passages, write and deliver sermons, counsel people who come to them, and administrate after a fashion. Often, they are overly introspective. Rarely have they been taught or required to reach out to people in the community. Many of these pastors boast that thay have the gift of preacher-teacher, and so do not need to "do the work of evangelism" as Paul commands Timothy (2 Timothy 4:5). Bereft of a model for hospitality, the church ministers to itself.

UNWILLINGNESS TO BE A SERVANT

Unwillingness to be a servant is another barrier

to hospitality. In the church, as in the world, Christians are attracted to and trained for the up-front, more visible jobs. The hidden back room tasks often go unattended to or are hastily slapped together. There is usually five to six hours of preparation and two to three hours of clean up for every hour of hospitality. Who wants that kind of servitude if we can opt for a more "public" kind of ministry with more affirmation?

NO DESIGNATED CADRE DOING OUTREACH
        Another barrier in reaching out is that all of the membership is often anchored to keeping the church organization functioning. Either our goal to reach out is so low on the priority list or our management techniques are so terrible that we cannot spare an outstretched hand to the outsider. Everybody is rowing so hard to keep the ship moving that we are often oblivious to the longing of the spectators along the shore. How can we see to it that, no matter how complicated and important our church organization becomes, a few of our people are released from the ongoing maintenance responsibilities to reach out in quality ways to new people?

IT FEELS SO COMFORTABLE INSIDE
        Still another problem slowing down the church's outreach is that many have been a part of things in

the church for so long—and it feels so good—that their ears are no longer hearing the symphony outside the church. We are so accustomed to the choir anthems that the music outside no longer touches us.

The first step for some of the people who became part of the Jonestown tragedy was that they didn't feel love in our Christian churches, Mel White writes in his book *Deceived*. One of the ex-Temple members, Jeannie Mills, expressed how her disillusionment began when she failed to receive support during a crisis in her life. As she visited many churches she couldn't find the warmth and acceptance she needed. Most hospitality consisted of the assembly-line hand shake with the pastor and the smile of a greeter. She didn't have the energy to break into the powerfully defined and existing church family. Nobody seemed to care in between Sundays until she went to People's Temple. After just one visit she was hugged, known by name, sent a box of candy from the church, and received *many personal* letters from parishoners.

DISTRUST OF THE VISITOR

Life in a competitive society tends to make reaching out more difficult and complicated. We may wonder—will this new person change things for me in my church?

—take my position on the board?

—require a little more of the pastor's time so I
   will get even less?

—create a need for yet another Sunday School
   teacher?

—change the church's priorities which I like as
   they are?

—dilute our church's faith?

As much as we "pounce on our visitors for the jobs
they can fill," even so we relate to them suspiciously
as an enemy to be careful of. For many of us there is
a love-hate relationship going with visitors.

When you think of new people coming into your
community, neighborhood, and church, what feelings
do they evoke? Write them down and reflect and
pray.

INABILITY TO MANAGE OUR TIME

Inability to manage our time looms as one of the
greatest obstacles in extending ourselves. My "to do"
sheet is never empty. There are so many "must"
items that the visitor has a difficult time gaining
entry. Few people evaluate my life on how I treat
strangers. *Who—but God— holds us accountable for
making room to include the outsider?*

Brainstorm about ways to clear your calendar
for one evening a month for the new folk with whom
you come in contact.

HOSPITALITY GETS CONFUSED WITH IMPRESSING PEOPLE

There is an idea that in order to be hospitable we have to be able to entertain people lavishly and put on a feast fit for a king. So, we take stock of our meager resources. We know that we are not as funny as Bill Cosby, nor can we afford the king's feast because we are not part owners of an oil well. Therefore, we are tempted to do nothing.

We need to remind ourselves that hospitality is not impressing people with our material resources and accomplishments: gourmet cooking, trophy room, spotless housekeeping, fancy location. Our calling is to love people.

IS MODERATION POSSIBLE?

One problem a few people face is a fear of excess. They are unable to assert themselves and say "no more," and so refrain from reaching out because they fear they cannot do it in moderation. They may have been burned in the past. The pastor called them to host *every* missionary the church had over a three-year period. Their parents gave so much time to strangers that they felt neglected as children. So, instead of brainstorming ways of achieving moderation or resolving the past, they simply refrain from *all* hospitality.

There is a great need to help each other

comprehend and interpret the biblical injunction to "be hospitable." How do we prevent people who are highly gifted in this area from being overwhelmed? The ancients had protection from hospitality exhaustion. They were to provide food and shelter and time-consuming acts for three days. But, if a guest was disposed to extend his stay beyond the "three days of grace," the host was to put him to work as one of the family.

I think today we need to dialogue creatively about our gifts so we are not destroyed by them. How long can a person teach in the church school program without a break? How long can one serve on the boards of the church without growing stale? Given my energy level and time available, how much hospitality can I give?

Henri Nouwen adds a refreshing realism to prevent hospitality compulsion. He gives me balance and relief from unnecessary guilt when I am not at a place where I can be hospitable.

> The movement from hostility to hospitality is a movement that determines our relationship to other people. We probably will never be free from all our hostilities, and there may even be days and weeks in which our hostile feelings dominate our emotional life to such a degree that the best thing we can do is to keep distance, speak little to others, and not

write letters, except to ourselves. Sometimes events in our lives breed feelings
of bitterness, jealousy, suspicion, and
even desire for revenge, which need time
to be healed . . . .[1]

BIGGER AND BETTER

Another trap to hospitality is that so few people
do it well that you can easily and quickly develop
quite a reputation. You become known as the person
who throws great parties. Each time you feel a
strange need to outdo yourself and live up to your
growing reputation. That can lead to a bigger or finer
house, better furniture, special equipment for youth
events, and on and on. Again, I believe we need the
Christian community to ask the questions, "When are
you simply meeting your ego needs?" and "When are
you seeking God's glory?"

USE BOTH HANDS

She was only five at the time. I was turning the
TV channel to find the World Series already in
progress and adjusting the color and the volume. My
little daughter was getting all dressed up for a birthday party. As I turned the color knob with one hand
I was unsuccessful in pulling up her zipper with my
other hand. Then there was a home run and the next
thing I remember my daughter was interrupting my
preoccupation by saying in her exasperated, little

adult manner, "Daddy! Use both hands." Hospitality is so often blocked by our preoccupation with other things.

We were having lunch together. I consider him one of my better friends. He lives some distance from me so such occasions are an anticipated treat. As I shared from the depths of my being a very painful struggle I was going through, he kept looking past me and not at me. I wanted to ask—"Are you interested in what I'm sharing?" A powerful barrier to hospitality is our lack of serious focus with people at hand.

A CULTURE THAT CANNOT INTERACT SOCIALLY

In some ways we live in a canned culture that cannot interact socially except in a pragmatic (official, business-like) way. We know how to take people to lunch to negotiate business contracts and bargain with office personnel and problem solve around a table. But what is the common evening for most of us? We go out to a meeting, attend a night class for updating our education, turn on the TV to unwind, or open our folder of material from the office to get caught up. Even our communication time in the family is carefully outlined:

—Car has broken down/I'll have it fixed Saturday

—Back bedroom needs painting/I'll try to do
    that on Saturday the 31st
—Community Theater Friday night/Would you
    please get the tickets?
We need help in the simple communication skills that
Marriage Encounter and other groups are teaching.
We have almost reached the point where we need "an
expert" to teach us how to have fun and play games
and enjoy effective social interaction.

THE PLUSH PAD
    If we have filled our home with fine china and
valuable artifacts, we will in most cases reduce our
possibilities for hospitality. We definitely wouldn't
want an "after the game" party to celebrate winning the championship. If we crowd that kind of
house with strangers, something will inevitably be
broken or stolen. As a youth minister for six years, I
always feared taking the youth to such delicate
homes. I dreaded something would be broken. My
fear was greatly reduced by the realization that we
were never invited to such a home. If we have a plush
pad, we can still reach out to a few select groups—but
many hospitality possibilities are eliminated.
    What obstacles would you add to this list of
things that keep you from reaching out to new people? As you reflect on these barriers, can you think
of ways to overcome them?

QUESTIONS FOR REVIEW AND DISCUSSION:

1. What are your barriers to practicing hospitality?

2. As you reflect on these barriers, can you think of ways to overcome them?

3. Discuss the barriers to practicing hospitality with a friend, and see if that input helps give you perspective.

4. Are you available for the menial kinds of tasks, or are you forever taking a front and center stage?

Spend some time in prayer about the subject of hospitality.

6

Brainstorming Possibilities for Hospitality

MY RESIDENCE AS A PLACE OF HOSPITALITY

How many homes does one look at before the purchase is made or a person decides to rent? How much time and energy is invested into making your home or apartment an expression of your personality and lifestyle? Reflect on a few ways that people show these different qualities: architecture, view, color, pictures, furniture, lighting, music, use of space, themes.

I have the privilege of visiting many homes in our community, and sometimes it reminds me of Disneyland. I go into *Tomorrowland* because the home seems ten years ahead of its time. Another home is like *Frontierland* with its Western theme. Some people have carried out themes from their heritage—a Japanese tea room; a little theater from years of collecting old movies; a basement in the

form of a submarine looking out from under the
swimming pool, reminscent of the owner's earlier
naval career; or the room with no chairs and everybody sitting on bean bags. It is a real *Adventureland.*

As stewards of our resources, we need to recon-
sider how it is that our homes belong to God. We
need to help each other process this most expensive
thing that God has entrusted to us.

For some, their home is their retreat. They
spend so much time and energy in their work that
they need to hide out to regain their strength. Others
see their home as a youth hostel. People are coming
and going all the time. Their children are bringing
home so many friends from college that many do not
even take the time to sign the guest register. Most of
us fall somewhere in between these two extremes.
How we use our homes as a resource for hospitality
is difficult and complicated. We need the Christian
community to help us think and pray and act upon
this matter.

Perhaps one beginning point is a service of dedi-
cation. Maybe we need to do something conscious
and deliberate to help it sink into our subconscious.
Here are some suggested prayers:

The house or apartment:
Father-God, bless this home (apartment).
May everyone here sense your presence.

Let your peace rest upon those who live
here, and those who visit.
May all who enter here sense your love
and feel your welcome.

The Living Room:
Father-God,
Touch this room with your love.
Permeate it with your presence so that
life can be shared at deeper levels—
in laughter and in tears,
in sickness and in health,
in good times and bad.
May people in this room listen to one
another,
share their plans and interests,
ideals and emotions,
caring for one another in deep
commitment.

The Kitchen:
Father-God,
May the preparation of food,
the kitchen clean up,
the informal conversation,
all the small acts of love done in this
room,
be a symbol always that we are your
servants,
And that you dwell with us.

The Bath:
Almighty God,
Water is also your gift to us:
a sign of cleansing,

the feeling of warmth,
the joy of being renewed.
Cleanse us, warm us, renew us,
that we may reach out to this world with
    love.

The Bedrooms:
Father-God, we recognize that "fatigue
    makes cowards of us all" and sleep is a
    source of strength in our lives.
So, grant to us the ability to put aside
    problems, pressures, and discomfort.
Give us all the deep peace with you that
    enables us to rest soundly,
So that we may return to your world
    each day
Awakened to your presence and alive to
    your call.[1]

Select a family symbol that expresses your
faith:
   —A *world map* because we are world citizens for
       Jesus Christ.
   —A *candle* that burns for 30 days, and is always
       replenished, symbolizing the light of Christ's
       presence among us.
   —A *cross* because we follow Jesus to our death.
   —An *open Bible* because we are a family of the
       Word.
   —A *family cup* because we share the cup of
       Christ's sorrow and joy.

—An *altar* where we worship the Lord daily and remember the importance of sacrificing ourselves for others.

—A *room* set aside specifically for prayer.

—*Special water* to remind us that we are a holy people.

—An *oil* to annoint our family for service.

—A *particular blessing* that symbolizes our family's life and mission.

—A *special greeting* at the door to welcome people.

—A *stake* or *marker* driven into the yard, which is our place and point of remembrance.

Maybe your family has need of a symbol that is less obviously religious but is made sacred by the way that you use it:

—A *coffee pot* always ready to perk up a discouraged neighbor.

—A *cookie jar* around which your children's friends gather.

—The *popcorn popper* which has everybody gathered around a common bowl.

—A *ping pong table* where people can laugh and shout and jump and play.

—The *dining room table* where people look into each other's faces and listen to each other and break bread together.

—A *drawer of maps* from which you plan your
next family vacation time together.

—*Jogging shoes, horseshoes, shuffleboard, swimming pool,* where everyone works out their
anxieties and hostilities.

—A *fireplace* where you dream dreams and feel
cozy and secure.

What is the symbol which best expresses your
family's faith and life together?

Wherever Abraham pitched his tent, he built an
altar to the Lord. That altar was a visible expression
of his worship of God and a constant reminder of his
values and priorities. On the other hand, no mention
is made of his nephew, Lot, symbolizing his faith in
God. The lives of Abraham and Lot proceeded in
vastly different directions. I often wonder how important Abraham's symbols were in contributing to
the difference. A person needs *meaningful* symbols in
his life that he has had a voice in choosing and bringing into being.

As a child, the church's symbols did not hold
meaning for me and no one helped me develop a set
of God-symbols. Thus, the symbols around which I
built my life drew me away from God rather than
toward him:

—my athletic letter sweater

—my scrapbook

—my cowboy boots

—my car

—my job

Now I am in the process of incorporating into my life
a series of symbols that integrate the presence and
call of Christ into my daily experience. It may be a
P.F. on my telephone, reminding me to "pray first"
before I answer the phone. Every time I hear a siren
from a police car or ambulance it has become a symbol to flash a five-second prayer of mercy for the
recipient.

You may be one who needs something more
than a prayer or a symbolic ritual to sense that "this
place where I live is a gift from God and it is available
for his purposes." Some people are really helped by
guided visualizations. Visualizations are a means of
perceiving hidden reality. You sit upright in a chair,
feet firmly on the floor. Place your hands in a comfortable position. Be aware of your breathing. Close
your eyes. Imagine a great light coming into your new
home through the front door. See in that light the
wonderful presence of God. Watch that light move to
each room—feel its comfortable warmth, its strength,
flowing with the light into each room, linger, and
finally return to your chair. Continue to reflect for
a moment on the presence of God right where you
live—"Where two or three are gathered in my name,
there I am in the midst of them,"[2] said Jesus. And,
again, "I am the light of the world."[3] When you are

ready, open your eyes and jot down any thoughts about this experience.

In growing up, my home was always a community center for my friends. Food was rarely served, but we were given space and freedom and friendship. My parents never had to guess who my friends were, where we went in our spare time, what we did when we were together. They just listened to all that was being discussed in their living room. Of course, that meant the furniture and rugs took a terrible beating. It meant our lawn had home plate and second base carved into it. Windows were replaced frequently because of foul balls breaking them. But my folks knew all the new young people who moved into our neighborhood and into my life.

THE COMMUNITY AS A RESOURCE FOR HOSPITALITY

The home is not everybody's place to show hospitality, and we should not be trapped into limiting this biblical term to receiving people into our homes. Because of health, location, abilities, or any number of things, many people need to select another place. Remember, hospitality is basically an attitude toward another person which can be expressed in many ways and places.

One of our favorite places to entertain people in our community is called the Grange. The Grange is an association of farmers that began in 1867 for their mutual welfare and advancement. As our community changes rapidly from rural to bedroom to urban, we have this great opportunity to give new people an experience of the best of twenty years ago. There is no way they can feel this at Denny's by the highway, or Sambo's on the main drag. There is always a handful of old farmers to reminisce on the *good old days*, a few people from the other churches, a place for the children to run and play, a visit from the cook, and a chance to watch her prepare your meal. We are free to give our total attention to our visitors.

One of the Christian men in our community invited all the dentists and their staffs to a private party at the new high school in anticipation of its opening in a couple of weeks. The administration and school board had a great opportunity for public relations. It was a unifying experience in the community.

What place in your city has intrigue and uniqueness to lend itself to Christian hospitality?

THE CHURCH AS A CENTER OF HOSPITALITY

The church is another logical center for hospitality. We are a large family—the family of God. Some people think that the church is one of the few places left where we can meet people who are different from us but form a larger family. It is amazing how we overlook the simple acts of hosting in the church:

—learning a person's name
—finding things for which to affirm them
—listening attentively
—introducing them to other people
—staying with them past the first hello
—making your name visible to them

The church needs to find more ways to take the visitor seriously. The church of which I am a part has periodic *friendship dinners*. People who have visited the church three or four times are invited into the home of a family in the church for dinner. There are twenty to thirty people, and the visitors outnumber the members (so that they have a balancing sense of power). The host is joined by the leaders of the church. It is made clear to the new people that they have the ear of the church leaders who need their input. What are their needs? What drew them to our church? What brought them back again? What is important to them? It is amazing, the helping that comes from a person who has not yet "settled in." When most church boards make decisions affecting new people, their only source of information is, "When I first joined this church seven years ago . . . ." We become out of touch, like the parent who keeps making all the decisions for his teenager by saying, "When I was your age . . . ." We have discovered that church visitors feel the "put-downs" even if they cannot verbalize them.

I have always been impressed by the late Methodist clergyman, Samuel Shoemaker. As busy as he became strengthening the inner life of a large church— writing books and speaking all over the country—he never lost sight of the newcomer. The following is a poem he wrote which is included in one of his books:

> I stand by the door,
> I neither go too far in, nor stay too far
>   out.
> The door is the most important door in
>   the world—
> It is the door through which men walk
>   when they find God.
> Men die outside that door, as starving
>   beggars die
> On cold nights, in cruel cities, in the
>   dead of winter.
> Nothing else matters compared to help-
>   ing them find it
> And open it, and walk in, and find Him
> So I stand by the door . . . .
>
> You can go in too deeply and stay in too
>   long,
> And forget the people outside the door.
> As for me, I shall take my old accus-
>   tomed place,
> Near enough to God to hear Him, and
>   know He is there,
> But not so far from men as not to hear
>   them,
> And remember they are there, too.

Where? Outside the door—
Thousands of them, millions of them,
But—more important for me—
One of them, two of them, ten of them,
Whose hands I am intended to put on
    the latch.
So I shall stand by the door and wait
For those who seek it.
"I had rather be a door-keeper . . . ."
So I stand by the door.[4]

Do not our churches need a dedicated cadre of people who emotionally and physically stand near the door with a heart open to new people and a commitment to minister to them over a long period of time?

Perhaps one of the reasons most main-line denominations are either just maintaining or losing membership is because there are no teams of people doing "friendship evangelism." One organization uses the term "pre-evangelism." They argue that there is a certain extending of ourselves and our resources to people *before* we communicate the gospel. And, if the church has no one doing pre-evangelism, the plans and programs and harvesting schemes of evangelism inevitably fall short.

Once upon a time there was a church in a beautiful location. As a body they demonstrated the gift of hospitality by building and decorating and furnishing one special room as pretty and functional and comfortable as a bank's hospitality room. They even made it available to other church staffs and boards for one-day use. Many churches have been refreshed, renewed, and encouraged by the farsighted vision and sacrifice of that one Carmel, California congregation. There is a need to think through what we as individuals can do to be hospitable, but also what we as a church can do collectively.

The church I serve has just selected and installed a large, magnificent stained glass window. It is a picture of Jesus Christ reaching out to receive the little children. We could have selected a picture of the Last Judgment, the angry warnings of John the Baptist, the stinging rebukes of the Old Testament prophets. We chose a picture depicting God in Jesus Christ as the gracious host welcoming us. Our children worship with us each week. We know visuals make a deep impression on their lives. We hope and pray that stained glass representation of God's character will draw them to the Savior and help them reach out to others in that same loving acceptance.

One church in which I worshiped had this ancient inscription carved in the narthex to remind everyone of the importance of reaching out to the stranger:

> In this little hour we
> Spend in fellowship with thee,
> Search us keenly, Lord, we pray
> Lest we leave thy house today

Through our stubbornness unfed
By the true and living bread
Lest we know not that we thirst.
   Selfishness we have nursed
   Through the years, O blessed Lord,
   Smite it with thy two-edged sword.
   Make us over, make us kind.
   Let no lonely stranger find
Lack of friendly handclasp, or
Pass unwelcome through the door.
Let the whole week sweeter be
For this hour we spend with thee.
                    Bertha G. Woods[5]

Each week the people were reminded of the needs of the lonely stranger and the priority of friendship.

Some years ago a writer in the *Los Angeles Times* visited numerous churches in the greater Los Angeles area and rated the friendship he experienced. The greeters at the door got 2 points. The prepackaged form letter from the pastor got 3 points. The coffee hour got about 5 points. Personal invitations to dinner were around 60 points. Introducing yourself in a cordial, non-threatening way was about 10 points. What numerical value would you give the different aspects of church hospitality? How would your church fare? How would you fare?

CHURCH LEADERS SET THE PACE FOR MODELING HOSPITALITY

A spirit of hospitality is an important quality in

a church leader. Paul writes to Timothy, "Now a bishop must be above reproach, the husband of one wife, temperate, sensible, dignified, hospitable" (2 Timothy 3:2). Again in Titus 1:7-8 we read, "For a bishop, as God's steward, must be blameless; he must not be arrogant or quick-tempered or a drunkard, or violent, or greedy for gain, but hospitable."

If the leaders of the church are commanded to be hospitable, what does this say about the general membership? Peter extends the responsibility of hospitality to all. "Practice hospitality ungrudgingly to one another" (1 Peter 4:9).

Those passages are a reminder that we are not free to exclude the left-out people from our lives and plans. The time and energy we invest in this area is most worthwhile.

THE ROMAN CATHOLIC CHURCH RETHINKS ITS MINISTRY TO THOSE ENTERING THE CHURCH

I have in my library a 151-page provisional book on the "Rite of Christian Initiation of Adults." It is a detailed study of how to treat new people in the church and prepare them for membership. The United States Catholic Conference reflects on what the church has done historically. They set their goals and develop symbols that will meaningfully express what they hope will happen. They breathe on the

candidate, symbolic of God breathing his Spirit upon
them. They place the sign of the cross on the fore-
head, symbolic of Christ's love and victory at Calvary.
They give them copies of the gospel which is the good
news of Jesus Christ. There is the anointing with the
oil of salvation, the enrollment of names, the func-
tion of godparents, presentation of lighted candles,
being clothed in a white garment . . . and other ways
to symbolize conversion, repentance, forgiveness, and
discipleship.[6]

OUR CHURCH REFLECTS ON HOW TO WEL-
COME NEW PEOPLE

We have begun discussions at all levels in our
church regarding what *we* want to communicate to
someone joining our church as he stands in front of
the congregation. How can we best say that? How
can we show it? We found in our study that we often
were not communicating what we wanted to communicate—warmth, acceptance, mutual commitment,
faith, witness, celebration. Rather, we were communicating coldness, interrogation, isolation. How did you
feel the day you joined the church standing in front
of the congregation answering questions propounded
by the pastor?

As we have placed ourselves in the shoes of a
stranger walking into our congregation on a Sunday
morning, we asked the question, "If God is a gracious

host, how can we as his representatives best invite people to come to him?" In five groups, I did not get one positive suggestion. They all told me how they did not want to be coerced or manipulated to come to God. They shared many embarrassing and negative experiences from childhood.

> —Those of you who want to come to God now, raise your hand.
> —Those of you who have raised your hand, stand up.
> —Those of you standing, come to the front.
> —Those of you in the front, follow Deacon Jones to the prayer room.

I understand that the above methods of asking for commitment are only about 300 years old, which is a short span in the history of the church. The scriptures do not require this particular form of invitation. I realize that sometimes these methods are very helpful, but at other times they are counter-productive. But new people who have become Christians in our church are asking me for some visual way to express that commitment—and they do not want to come forward, and say they would not have. How do we meet their need?

I hope you now see that I believe brainstorming possibilities for hospitality in the church should not be limited to greeters before service, or a coffee hour after the last service, but should include *everything* we do.

POSSIBILITIES FOR HOSPITALITY IN MY
OCCUPATION

The challenge in our place of occupation is to be
efficient and productive, which is what we are paid
for. Also, we need to be sensitive to people and not
trample on them or treat them as impersonal ma-
chines. This calls for some creative dialogue among
Christians.

I have met numerous secretaries whose simple
candy dish was the center of warmth in a large office. I have seen others whose flower arrangements
did the same thing in their places of business. Still
another had a cartoon-filled bulletin board—the only
place in a pressure-filled company where people feel
free to laugh and be themselves. Some persons have
so developed an ability to give genuine affirmation
and encouragement that they have become the unof-
ficial host or hostess of the office. Still others, by the
sheer force of their personalities, have been able to
change the pervading mood of the office from hostility to friendliness. Hospitality can become a life-style,
and not something we turn on and off at church.

Some choose to do their entertaining through
the growing popularity of the athletic club. They take
visitors over for physical exercise, a relaxed sauna, a
hot tub experience, and a bite of lunch or dinner.
Others see their cabin as a place for ministry. They
make it available to the youth group so that visiting

young people can be integrated into the life of the group. It is hard to get young people to be friendly with their peers in just one to three hours of contact per week. A retreat experience where there are close personal relationships over a period of two or three days can become the place for new young people to really feel a part of the group. Women's groups in the church find a cabin an excellent place to take new women for friendship building.

QUESTIONS FOR REVIEW AND DISCUSSION:

1. How do you view your home? Is it your castle? or your retreat center? or??

2. Have you ever consciously dedicated your home to God?

3. What is a good symbol of your family?

4. What is it in your city that has intrigue and/or uniqueness—to lend itself to Christian hospitality?

5. How can your church take visitors more seriously?

6. In your place of occupation, how do you exercise hospitality?

7. Do you belong to any service clubs or commun-
    ity organizations that enable you to demonstrate
    friendship?

8. Are the homes of the members of your church
    open or closed to one another?
    How would you rate the climate or community
    in your congregation?

7

Effects of Hospitality

STORIES OF HOW HOSPITALITY AFFECTED
PERSONAL LIVES

Hospitality has had tremendous effects on the
world as well as individuals. Historians tell us that
hostels and hotels and inns grew out of hospitality.
As people came to shrines, they needed places to stay
so the early hostels grew out of that movement. Many
of these people were sick, and so the hostels were
turned into hospitals. The whole hospital movement
owes its inception to hospitality.

A young friend of mine took a summer to visit
colonies of Hutterites and Mennonites all across Can-
ada and the United States. After spending a number
of days or weeks with each group, one common
quality emerged among them. It permeated everything they did. It reflected in the way they treated
him. Steve said it has permanently changed his life.

What was that quality? "Friendship is sacred!" Today he is affiliated with a community, building friendships and extending friendship to other people.

I wonder how many people reading this book have met Jesus Christ personally through a Young Life or Campus Life Club that met in someone's home week after week? How many people across the country open their homes each week, watch all their living room furniture carried out, see the room fill with wall-to-wall teenage bodies, listen to the gospel presentation, wave good-bye to departing kids, return the furniture to the proper place, breathe a quick prayer of gratefulness, and a sigh of relief? Only God can measure such an immense weekly impact because of home hospitality.

How many college students find the Lord each year because another student opens her room for study and rap times? How many churches in our country which are now elaborately decorated and marvelously functional owe their beginnings to somebody's living room?

As I talk with older pastors, many of them tell me that their greatest training was in the open homes of their seminary professors, not in the classroom. Of course, that was before the days of expanded accreditation rules and the "publish or perish" syndrome. I can remember the sign on the door of the office of one of my prolific writer-professors, "Please don't bother me unless your problem is urgent. I am a very busy man." And very few students bothered him—or were touched by his life and teaching.

When I look back on the profound influences in my life, one was a youth minister who took me to dinner with visiting Christians such as Henrietta Mears, founder of Gospel Light Press and Forest Home Conference Center, Major Ian Thomas, director of the Torchbearers in England, J. Edwin Orr, an evangelist, Dr. John Wolvord, president of Dallas Seminary, Bill Bright, founder and director of Campus Crusade for Christ, and Donald Grey Barnhouse, prominent writer, pastor, and theologian. The friendship around the dinner table increased the intensity of my desire to hear them speak and read their books.

The late Dawson Trotman, founder of the Navigators, tells the story of seeking to make his home a center of hospitality from the beginning of his marriage. Within three or four years' time a sailor from every state in the union had found Christ as Savior and Lord in their living room.

One of the more fruitful times in my ministry was the five years we had a little, old, run-down cabin in the hills an hour from our church. I took small groups of students every other weekend to simply study the scriptures and build friendships. I could do more in one weekend than in weeks of one-hour sessions on Sunday morning. New students were integrated into the group in one weekend, whereas it would have taken three to six months of Sunday mornings. My guess is that many of them would never have stayed the many months and endured those pressures until they were known, trusted, and accepted.

One of the most hospitable mothers I know said the effects of their community outreach upon her children were profound. Her children are mature for their ages because they listened to college students debate issues, Christian leaders address all sorts of problems, and couples work on their marriages. She traces her children's ability and comfortableness in expressing themselves with all ages and all kinds of people to the many people who have been in their home. The children developed a life style of reaching out because their parents had modeled it, and they felt comfortable doing it in the security of their own home. Because of multiple models in their home, she feels her children expanded their interests, gifts, and abilities beyond what they would normally have done had not so many guests been a part of their household.

UNEXPECTED BLESSINGS OF HOSPITALITY

One of the unexpected blessings of hospitality is that the senior citizen can be included and can reciprocate in helpfulness. My pastor-friend has had a staff of six to eight college students working in his church every summer for the past twenty years. Though the staff has different responsibilities and goes in many different directions, at noon each day they all eat together. His mother and aunt, well past the age of 65, have an incredible ministry doing all the cooking and baking. Their prayer life has been deepened. They have not stopped growing as persons. They are in touch with the fast-changing world of young people. The federally mandated retirement age has not affected them. Their vital contribution makes much of his ministry possible.

Another unexpected blessing is that the stranger brings gifts, but can't give them until he is freed from his strangeness and welcomed as a fellow human being. Two men were walking down the road one day, discussing the dramatic events of the crucifixion and resurrection, when they were joined by a third person who entered into their conversation. Some time later they invited this stranger to join them for dinner and, in the breaking of the bread, he made himself known—the resurrected Lord Jesus (Luke 24: 13-35). Elijah, the prophet, received hospitality from the widow of Zarephath. In return, he gave her an abundance of oil and meal, and raised her son from the dead (I Kings 17:9-24). Granted, not every stranger we befriend will return such dramatic miracles, but, as Christians, we believe that every meeting of persons is an exchange of gifts. If we pass as strangers in the night, we rob each other of blessings.

QUESTIONS FOR REVIEW AND DISCUSSION:

1. What do you think it means to call friendship
    sacred?

2. Have you ever experienced an unexpected bles-
    sing from a stranger whom you made a friend?

3. What are some other ways to include children
    and adults in hospitality?

❧ 8 ❧

Helpful Hints

KEEP IT SIMPLE

There is an old chestnut that ministers often tell. A little church in the midwest got a young man and his wife just out of seminary to be their pastor. Each week as the new minister went into the pulpit his wife, sitting in the front row, would whisper—"Kiss, kiss, kiss." At first the congregation was thrilled with the young bride's enthusiasm. But, as it continued week after week, and month after month, they became annoyed. Finally, one lady was appointed to speak to the minister's wife. She approached the young lady and said, "We in the church appreciate your affection for your husband, but why must you say lovingly every time he goes to the pulpit, "Kiss, kiss, kiss?" The pastor's wife replied, "It isn't affection at all. It means 'Keep it simple, stupid'."

In entertaining—we need to keep it simple.

Gourmet meals are not essential. Meals do not need to be expensive and they do not have to take a great amount of time and energy to prepare. Perhaps you can invite people to a dessert only. Or, it can be delicious soup which is bought from a nearby delicatessen. Or, it can be a do-it-yourself salad bar luncheon for our weight-conscious generation. Simplifying your food preparation will give you more time to focus on your guests.

LET YOUR NEW FRIENDS PARTICIPATE

If someone volunteers to help, let them bring a dessert or help with one or two things when they arrive. That might be a bridge-builder to friendship that cannot be accomplished in a more formal sit-down conversation. If someone is willing to clear the table, or wash a dish or two, why not let them? It can help them feel more deeply involved in the event. It can be a means of affirmation for what they have done. It can help you keep your entertainment expenses down.

ACCENT THE UNIQUENESS OF YOUR APART— MENT OR HOME

What drew you to the place where you are living? Was it the entry way? an extra big family room? a kitchen with a spectacular view? a balcony? a big yard? What have you done to make those things extra special? Can you share that with friends? Have you visited that very old home in the inner city that is filled with antiques? Or visited a home with a large picture window looking out on a massive oak tree? The uniqueness of such places are more apparent, but everyone can learn to make their hospitality more interesting by accenting the unique features of their abodes.

SET HOSPITALITY GOALS FOR YOURSELF

Perhaps you will begin to aim for a once-a-month occasion to extend yourslf to new persons. Plan it into your budget. You might even put something in your cooker before church, praying that you will meet a guest. Pray that God will bring someone into your life whom you can befriend in the name of Christ.

Another helpful hint that a number of people have shared with me is to always have on hand the ingredients for a favorite dish which can be fixed easily and quickly. In my bachelor days, a friend taught me how to make spaghetti sauce in thirty minutes with just hamburger and tomato soup and a few spices from the cabinet. It doesn't taste like a professional chef's sauce, but it passes for a good meal. And, of course, I prepare it with dramatic fanfare. I put on a chef's hat, line up all the ingredients, make lots of noise, add many extra movements, and have

great fun. The novelty of seeing me cook the one
meal I do three times a year adds to the occasion.
This meal is not only fun, it is inexpensive. Spaghetti
is also one of the few meals that is a favorite of everyone in our family. What simple, inexpensive meal can
you have ready for a spur-of-the-moment occasion?

My father's hobby was trout fishing in the
streams of Lake Superior. Our freezer always had a
couple of five-to-eight-pound trout. As company
came, the big fish was taken out and thawed and
filled with lots of butter. To company, ours was the
home of frequent delicious fish dinners. And they
heard the story of the fish that was caught, rather
than the one that got away.

Janelle is a mother of two small children, teaching two art classes, and selling her paintings commer-
cially. She was also making and selling stained glass
windows. In between times she led a Bible study and
visited people in their homes on a regular basis. Somehow, she still managed to have numerous groups of
people new to our community into her home for
dinner parties. I interviewed her and this is what I
learned.

1) Clean the house the day before. If you take
on scrubbing, washing and ironing, cupboard
arranging, grocery shopping, plus cooking in
the same day, you'll be too tired to enjoy the
evening. *The enjoyment has to outweigh the
effort.*

2) Make a list of things to do with a corresponding time schedule—

a) prepare the main course   4:00 p.m.
b) set the table   5:00 p.m.
c) potatoes in the oven   5:30 p.m.
d) salad   5:45 p.m.
e) change clothes   6:00 p.m.
f) heat the bread   6:15 p.m.
g) greet the guests   6:30 p.m.

3) Determine your goal beforehand. Why are you reaching out to these people? If married, it helps for it to be a common goal with your spouse.

4) Accept people where they are on that particular evening. If they want to engage in intellectual conversation, fine. If they want to crack jokes and laugh and release tensions, okay. If they prefer to be quiet and reflective, let them.

I remember the following lesson on hospitality from my own childhood: My father spent an hour before company arrived reading through twelve articles in the *Reader's Digest*. The people visiting our home felt he was one of the most interesting conversationalists they had ever met. He always had many topics fresh and alive in his mind because of that simple exercise.

Another gracious hostess, the wife of an execu-

tive in our community, shared her keys to hospitality
with me. She said she practiced meeting her guests at
the door before they actually came. She also said she
practiced introducing them to each other so her intro-
ductions would be crisp and clear and confident,
rather than faltering and embarrassing. People always
enjoy being in her home. They postpone vacations
and cancel other obligations to be guests at her home
for dinner.

There is a man with a great ability to relax people. Everyone seems comfortable in his home. I certainly do. He is so naturally funny that I envy his
ability to be humorous. One day he confided to me
that he read from joke books and humorous story
books for thirty minutes the day the company was
coming. He found several good jokes and told them at
work until he selected the best one or two. He has
worked at that for fifteen years. That little discipline
served as the evening icebreaker and relaxed the
company.

A SIMPLE GIFT

One of my friends gardens for a hobby. He be-
longs to a small, growing church. Every Saturday he
takes flowers from his garden and transplants them
into pretty, inexpensive pots. He either visits the
home of people who have come to worship the week
before, or has them come to dinner. Each family is

given the potted flower. "We are a beautiful, alive, and growing church," he explains. "As the attractive plant grows, may it remind you of us. As the flower multiplies, divide it and give half to a friend. We hope it will symbolize our faith. We enjoy giving our faith away. We hope you will pass it on too."

A GUIDE TO INTERNATIONAL FRIENDSHIP
Some years ago, Inter-Varsity Christian Fellowship published an excellent little booklet by Paul Little to stimulate Christians to reach out to international students. He had a section on the international students' desire for personal friendship in depth, desire to learn, interest in Christianity, and misunderstandings about Christianity including conceiving of Christians as superficial. I was really helped by his practical suggestions on how to establish contact, how to develop a friendship, and how to share your faith. I quote his "Tips for Hosts."

An invitation should be clear and definite. If possible, call for the student at his residence.

It is most essential to learn to pronounce the person's name correctly in advance. If you're not quite sure, ask him to write it out and to pronounce it for you so you can practice it until you can say it correctly.

It is usually better to invite two students for the first visit rather than just one, since they're much more at ease with another friend present. It's often good to invite a student who has been previously entertained in the home, along with a new guest.

It is important to realize that students from certain backgrounds have dietary restrictions. Moslems and Jews do not eat any kind of pork or ham, and could be quite offended if it were served in their presence. Hindus and Buddhists often do not eat beef; some may be strict vegetarians. Lamb, chicken, and scale fish are the most universally accepted forms of meat to serve. It may be that your particular guest may not practice any of these restrictions, but it's best to observe them for the first visit and then to inquire as to whether they are observed.

Rice is a staple food all over the Far and Middle East. Students from these areas very much appreciate the opportunity to eat it. You can easily learn from the students what kinds of food they prefer. Don't force them to eat or urge them to eat things that may not appeal to them. However, in some cultures it is impolite to accept the first invitation to have more, and food should be offered more than once.

Don't feel you must entertain elaborately. Students appreciate anything that is done nicely for them. Generally, they don't like to be considered as special guests but prefer to fit into the regular routine.

Be sure to invite the student back. Students for the most part are frustrated by one-time experiences and would like to penetrate more deeply into American life through the eyes of one person or family that they can get to know well. The student may feel he has failed in some way if he is not invited back a second time.

Above all, be spontaneous and never look upon a student as a curiosity. Approach your guest in the spirit of the learner.[1]

PLANNING THE MOOD

Another positive thing we can do in entertaining

is to think through the mood. The hostess sets the mood for successful interaction by having the lighting soft, but not dim; providing for movement and ventilation; using background music that is soft enough to allow for comfortable conversation.

PLANNING YOUR FOCUS

We had the people from the Community Services Division of our county come and teach us more about entertaining. Here is an insert taken from their training booklet which they have encouraged me to pass along to you also.

Unless the guests are all well acquainted and already have mutual interests, a party needs a purpose. The following examples allow guests to get acquainted by focusing on what is happening during the course of the party.

1. Coffee Tasting - Provide attractive cups, unusual coffee blends.

2. Costumes - The costume party gives the guests something to talk about. Even more fun is the social event where the guests create their own costumes with materials provided by the host/hostess. Hats may be substituted for full costumes and joke prizes add to the festivities.

3. Parties with a purpose - Invite people who are sympathetic to the same cause and provide an activity that supports that issue. An example of this type of get-together is a party where the guests decorate Easter eggs for the Crippled Children's Society.

4. Activities - Most people shy away from the word "games" but planned activities can be substituted for themes. Below are several suggestions of things to do.

Mixer 1: Pin a picture of some item or person on each guest's back. Using only yes or no questions, guests determine what is on their back.

Mixer 2: This activity is called "Murder!" Each guest is asked to draw a slip of paper from a hat, a small bowl, or other container. The person who draws the "M" is the Murderer. The "M" kills by winking. The persons killed should let a moment lapse before declaring themselves dead. See how many people the "M" can get before being spotted by any of the other players.

Mixer 3: Dictionary Game. Supplies:

paper, pencils, and a dictionary. There should be four players or more. A person is selected to be the "dictionary" for the first game and then this honor rotates to each other player in turn.

The person who holds the dictionary selects an obscure word and verbalizes it. No one should previously know the word. The "dictionary" then spells the word and everyone copies it down on his piece of paper. Then everyone constructs his own definition privately, and turns it in to the leader (folded or face down).

Meanwhile, the person holding the dictionary writes the actual definition on a piece of paper and includes it in the pile of definitions. When everyone has submitted their definition, the leader reads each one aloud and everyone votes on which is the correct one.

Scoring: Each person who chooses the correct definition gets ten points. Every time someone selects your definition (when you aren't the "dictionary") you get two points.

The "dictionary" rotates to the next person and the play resumes.

5. Entertainment may be substituted for activities with a group that tends to be more passive and reluctant to get involved.[2]

Their training goes on to give examples of appetizers, alternate beverages, and suggestions for ending the evening's festivities. If their premise is right (and I think it is), that creative entertaining can play a role in reducing alcohol abuse, it signals a great opportunity for Christians. I am my brother's keeper, and sometimes that means confronting him with his problem. At other times it means structuring more helpful situations.

Appetizers

Please note that the recipes provided here are not salty and some contain a sweet addition, such as sweet pickle or chutney. Serving very salty appetizers like chips and dip, salty pretzels, or bacon spread will increase thirst and guests will want to drink more. On the other hand, if guests are served appetizers such as vegetables with herb dip or fresh fruit and sour cream, cheese-stuffed mushrooms or broiled shrimp, the desire for alcohol will diminish.

Fresh Fruit Topiary Tree
A topiary tree of fresh fruit chunks or balls attached to a styrofoam base with decorative picks makes an edible and attractive centerpiece.

Curry Dip
½ cup sour cream
½ cup mayonnaise
1 tsp (or more) curry
1 tsp dried onion flakes
2-3 drops Tabasco

Mix all ingredients together and serve with raw vegetables of your choice.

Vegetable Dip
1 pint cottage cheese
½ cup mayonnaise
1 tsp Beau Monde seasoning
½ tsp dill
½ tsp Worcestershire sauce
dash of pepper
1 tsp parsley flakes
1 tsp chopped chives
Paprika to sprinkle on top

Mix all ingredients together and serve with raw vegetables of your choice.

Cheese Balls
2 cups grated sharp cheese
1 cup flour
2/3 cube melted butter
2 drops Tabasco
½ tsp paprika

Mix all ingredients and wrap around stuffed green olives or pieces of frankfurters. Place on cookie sheet and freeze. Heat for 20 minutes at 400 degrees.

Asparagus Ham Swirls
8 tsp mustard
2 pkg (6 oz each) cooked ham slices
2 pkg sliced Swiss cheese
16 cooked (or canned) asparagus spears
2 eggs beaten
1 cup dried bread crumbs
Oil for frying

Spread mustard on each ham slice, top with cheese. Place asparagus across one end, roll up (jelly roll) and secure with toothpick. Dip each roll in beaten eggs, then dip in crumbs. Fry in 1 inch of hot oil until brown. Drain on towels. Cut each roll into 3 pieces. Keep warm in oven as prepared. Makes about 48 appetizers.

Stuffed Mushrooms
1 lb fresh mushrooms with stems
3 green onions, chopped
½ tsp Worcestershire sauce
½ tsp garlic salt
2 tbsp milk
1 tsp parsley
Salt and pepper to taste
8 oz pkg cream cheese
1 pkg Good Seasons Blue Cheese
   Dressing Mix

Clean and remove stems from mushrooms. In butter, slightly saute tops, remove and drain upside down on paper towel. In same butter, saute stems. Remove from butter and chop. Mix all ingredients together and stuff mushroom caps, sprinkle with paprika. Refrigerate until ready to serve, then broil until hot and bubbly, 3-5 minutes (watch carefully!).

Cheese Squares
¾ lb sharp cheese, grated
1½ cube butter, softened
2-3 drops Tabasco
1 tsp Worcestershire sauce
1 tsp garlic salt
1 loaf unsliced white bread

With cheese at room temperature, beat first five ingredients in large bowl with mixer until smooth. Cut off crust of bread; cut into 1 inch cubes and freeze. When frozen, spread with cheese mixture on all sides; place on cookie sheet and freeze again. When ready to use, heat for about 15 minutes at 350 degrees.

Beverages

The following recipes for non-alcoholic beverages are attractive and delicious.

Iced Coffee Trinidad
Glass of iced coffee
2-3 dashes bitters
Small scoop chocolate ice cream
Mix all in glass. Serves 1.

Espresso Cream

2 cups water
9 squares sweet cooking chocolate
1 stick cinnamon
2 tbsp sugar
4 tsp instant espresso coffee
½ cup whipped cream
ground cinnamon

Heat first four ingredients in saucepan until chocolate melts. Stir in coffee until it dissolves. Pour into demitasse cups and sprinkle with ground cinnamon. Serves 6.

Hilty Dilty

½ oz Grenadine
½ oz lime juice
Dash (maybe ½ tsp) apricot syrup or flavoring

Mix together and pour over crushed ice. Fill glass with ginger ale, 7-Up, or soda. Serves 1.

Citrus Punch

1 (12 oz) can frozen orange juice
1 (12 oz) can frozen lemonade
3 cups water
1 tbsp bitters
1 (28 oz) bottle ginger ale or 7-Up

Mix all ingredients together and serve. Makes 12 six ounce cups.

Frozen Daiquiris
1 (6 oz) can lemon lime juice
2½ cans water
1 tsp artificial rum flavoring

Put all ingredients in blender filled with ice and mix. Serves 4. Note: for fruit daiquiris you can add any fruit such as strawberries, bananas, pineapple, etc.

Hot Orange Mocha
1 small orange
6 cups strong coffee
1 cup instant cocoa mix
½ cup whipping cream
1 tbsp sugar
¼ tsp vanilla

Pare orange rind thinly, combine with coffee and simmer 5 minutes. Remove and discard rind. Stir in cocoa mix. Pour into large mugs. Whip cream with sugar and vanilla; float dollop of cream on top. Serves 6.

Eggnog
6 egg yolks
¾ cup sugar
1/8 tsp salt
1 tbsp bitters
6 egg whites, stiffly beaten
4 cups hot milk
nutmeg

Beat yolks with ½ cup sugar, salt, and
bitters until fluffy. Add remaining sugar
into stiffly beaten egg whites, fold into
first mixture. Gradually stir in hot milk.
Pour into mugs; sprinkle with nutmeg.

Suggestions for Ending the Evening's Festivities

When it is time for the party to begin drawing to
a close, the thoughtful host/hostess can signal the
guests by serving coffee, tea, juice, dessert, or—

"Party's Over" Soup
4 cans beef consomme
2 cans French onion soup
1 tsp dried parsley
1 tsp fine herbs
4 tbsp cooking sherry

Heat all ingredients to boiling and add
cooking sherry. Boil several more minutes to remove alcohol content from the
soup. Pour in insulated mugs and sprinkle with grated Parmesan cheese and another dash of parsley.

BE READY ALWAYS TO CELEBRATE!

One reason the Christian community is slow to
celebrate is because the events sneak up on us and are
gone before we are prepared to enjoy them—retirement of a friend, moving of a dear neighbor, promo-

tion of someone at work, graduation of a nephew, baptism of someone we know, a drop-in guest, restoration of a broken relationship, visit to the grandparents, etc. In the biblical account of the Prodigal Son the father had a fatted calf ready for a happy occasion, which turned out to be the return of his son. How great to have a dad who is always ready for something wonderful to happen. Perhaps you need a file of congratulations cards or happy birthday cards so that you can do in five minutes what you do not do because of an hour's effort at the local card shop. Be ready to celebrate. You never know when the King of all the universe will tap you on the shoulder to pull off something really exciting. Stock the freezer and the pantry and your writing desk with the things you need for celebrating.

QUESTIONS FOR REVIEW AND DISCUSSION:

1. What practical suggestions would you give to another host or hostess?

2. What practical suggestions would you give for making hospitality easier?

3. How can you accent the uniqueness of your residence?

4. What can you do to increase your comfort level with guests?

9

Hospitality at a Time of Grief

"I feel so helpless!" Have you heard yourself express those words at the news of a friend's death? It is of vital importance for a grieving family to know that friends care. Attending a funeral or memorial service is one way you meet that need. Your very presence at the service can bring comfort. You are giving two precious things—your time and energy. It takes energy to go through the emotional drain of a funeral service. Your simple attendance communicates that you want to stand with those who are in sorrow today. I have always been amazed at how well grieving persons can remember weeks and months later the individuals who were at the funeral service. Reading the names from the guest register book can bring tears of love and comfort to the grieving family days after the funeral.

There are many other expressions of love and

comfort. Some people send flowers. Others make a memorial contribution. Still others send cards, letters, or bring food to the home. There are a number of ways to share the grief and ease the pain. In these little acts we are symbolically offering our love and pledging our concern.

TOWARD BETTER UNDERSTANDING THE FEELINGS OF A GRIEVING PERSON

At a time of death many emotions are intensified and are often in conflict. There can be guilt or fear or anger or disappointment or regret—all screaming for attention and resolution at the same time. We hear ourselves or others say, "If only I had said this . . . or "If only I had done this . . . ." Now what can we do at such a time? First, we need to affirm that it is normal to have such feelings and it is all right to express them. You may be one of the few friends who allows a grieving person to do this.

The Psalmist found resolution and comfort in knowing that God cared about him.

> For as the heavens are high above the
>   earth,
>   so great is his steadfast love toward
>   those who fear him;
>   as far as the east is from the west,
>   so far does he remove our transgres-
>   sions from us.

As a father pities his children,
   so the Lord pities those who fear him.
For he knows our frame;
   he remembers that we are dust.
                              Psalm 103:11-14

GRIEF IS NOT HEALED IN AN INSTANT!

Some of us are more reflective in our expressions of love. We have to process a tragedy for a few days before we can act. We deal first with our numbness, then with our own fears, and get in touch with our deepest feelings many days later. Often, we feel it is too late to act because a week or two has passed. But actually the opposite is true. God may have a special ministry of hospitality for you. After the first few days most people have forgotten or will be back in the busy routine of living. If the healing process is to continue, someone must go on caring. You can ask the questions: How can I relieve the loneliness of the family this week? How can I give practical proof of my love next month and next year when, regrettably, many will have forgotten?

MORE HELP IN PROCESSING GRIEF
Relationally

In grief let us
Put our arms around each other;

> In joy let us
> Sing and dance together;
> In life let us
> Celebrate our health;
> In death let us
> Celebrate our hope.

One important thing we can do is to communicate to grieving people that they are not alone. They need to know someone is available when the relatives have gone home and the neighbors have stopped cooking. When they are sitting home alone and the emptiness comes, they need to know that the people of God care for them. It is not so much what we say but the act of being present.

It is often in trusting relationships that we express our grief. So another thing we can do is to help people to express what they are feeling. Jesus, as he faced death, did this very thing in crying out to his Father. Acknowledging his feelings helped him to work them through and come to acceptance. Depending upon where a person is with the Lord, we can bring hope through the resurrection of Christ. Therefore, we can bring an added dimension to sorrow—the celebration of our hope.

Friendships can be deepened during a time of grief and things shared that are very personal. Therefore, we need to guard a person's privacy. Genuine hospitality carries the principle of trust. Trust is strengthened by keeping confidences. In grief we put our arms around each other. What more can be said than "I'm sorry" or "I love you." Therefore, touch becomes a very important way of communicating. In fact, during a period of grief is the only time some people feel free enough to hug or be hugged. Rubbing the shoulders can release tension and communicate love and support.

Psychologically

There has been a great deal of study over the past few years on the emotional adjustments of grief. Here is an abbreviated outline of the stages of grief most people experience. The St. Thomas Community of Christians in Visalia, California, gives this outline to each family going through grief:

Shock and Denial

"It can't be true!" You are shocked by the death of a loved one. You want to deny it, to block it out of your consciousness. You may feel numb and think the world is unreal. After numbness passes, you begin to grieve. Crying is good and important for you. A good cry helps to release the emotional pressure. Relatives should not try to stop your tears or insist that you be given a shot or tranquilizer unless your family doctor advises it.

Intense Mourning

You pine and yearn for the dead; wishing for the loved one's return. You may often dream of his/her return. You may expect the return at a certain time of the day. There may be acute feelings of anxiety and pain.

You may sense anger: sometimes a mild protest; sometimes a rage. You may feel angry towards the persons who cared for the deceased during his/her final illness; sometimes against God; against relatives over remarks or actions; against, even, the deceased who seemed to abandon you. Anger sometimes produces guilt, especially when you have been taught that feelings of anger against loved ones are not acceptable.

Guilt is present in most cases since, after the death of a relative, we no longer can deal directly with that person. The grieving person sometimes feels responsible for the death. Most often guilt is experienced as one remembers the things that were not done for the deceased.

The mourner may be preoccupied
with a sense of loss and loneliness. Time
drags; days are long and nights, longer.
The focus is on one's self and not on the
deceased. This feeling may lead to recovery.

Depression comes and goes. At times
it may seem impossible to do the routine
tasks. You may not have the energy or
desire.

Recovery and Readjustment

The final stage is a process of extended and gradual recovery. It may last
from six months to a year. However,
each person recovers at his/her own
pace. Friends to whom you may hon-
estly express your feelings are most important and helpful. It would seem ill
advised to rush too soon into many new
activities or make major changes in your
life style. Mourning has, as its object,
freeing the grieving person from dependence on the deceased. If the bond is
ended too soon, or if the dependence
continues too long, the mourner may
suffer ill effects. If you are still having
trouble getting over your grief after one
year, it may be good to seek professional
counseling.[1]

What is helpful to remember is that throughout each of these stages, the healing power of the Lord is ever present for the asking. Here is a possible prayer:

Lord, help me to remember that nothing
is going to happen to me today that you
and I can't handle together.

Theologically

A greeting card I once read communicated something very important to the grieving person:

It is comforting to know
    that God will not forsake you,
        and that friends are standing by.

Grieving people need to know that God is still with them. When Israel was in captivity in Babylon, they grieved because they thought God had abandoned them. The prophets' message to Israel was that God had not abandoned them. That proclamation gave the captives hope. After the resurrection and before the ascension Jesus reassured his disciples, "Lo, I am *with you always*, even to the close of the age." Grieving people need that message of the reality of Christ's presence. One universal attraction to the twenty-third Psalm is that even in the valley of the shadow of death, we can be assured that the Shepherd goes with us. Here are some suggested readings from the Bible:

Comfort and Hope
Psalm 23
Psalm 39
Romans 5:12-17
1 Corinthians 15:21-22
When feeling guilty about death
1 John 1:9
Ephesians 1:7
Isaiah 1:18, 44:22
When doubting the love of God
Jeremiah 29:11-13
Acts 17:27-28
Victory over bodily death
Romans 8
Philippians 1:21-23
1 Corinthians 15
2 Corinthians 5:1-4
Readings from the Gospels
Death and resurrection of Jesus: Luke
23:44-49, 24:1-5
No one who believes in Jesus will be
lost: John 6:27-40
Jesus and the death of Lazarus, a
friend: John 11:17-27

HOW DO I PRAY?

One simple prayer out of a denominational prayer book reads like this:

> O Lord: support us all the day long, until the shadows lengthen and the evening comes, and the busy, busy world is hushed, and the fever of life is over, and our work is done. Then in your mercy grant us a safe lodging and a holy rest, and peace at the last, through Jesus Christ our Lord.

Here is another prayer:

> Our Father
> Comfort these loved ones. Watch over them in the days ahead.
> When they are hurting, bring them healing,
> When they are lonely, comfort them.
> Strengthen their faith in you, O God, and in our Lord, Jesus Christ in order that they might follow Christ in the resurrection from the dead and the sure hope of eternal life. Amen.

Here is yet another simple prayer:

> Stand by those who sorrow that as they lean upon your word, they may find hope and strength and comfort. In Jesus' name, Amen.

QUESTIONS FOR REVIEW AND DISCUSSION:

1. What expressions of love and comfort have you received at a time of grief?

2. Which were most helpful to you?

3. What does your church do to help grieving persons? Immediately? After the services? A few weeks or months later?

❧ 10 ❧

The Necessity of Reaching Out

I heard one of the leaders of the Christian church speak about his experience at the Moonie's (followers of Sun Myung Moon) Unification Theological Seminary in Barrytown, New York.

He said one of the major attractions to the Moon cult is that they really *honor* education. In America many segments of our society distrust, or at best tolerate, our educated young people. Along comes a group of Moon's people who deeply respect their intellectual search and pilgrimage, and know how to honor them in the best of Oriental customs. Should we be surprised when some bright young college people leave everything—friends, family, possibilities of big salaries—and join the Moonies for acceptance—value—purpose—discipline—meaning—answers—community?

One of the great attractions to Mormonism is

the hospitality of their people. I have talked exten-
sively with two young people who were joining the
Mormon Church, not because the theology made
sense, but because their own Christian homes and
many families in the Christian community were in
disarray and a Mormon family had welcomed them
week after week into their home.

God has carved the necessity for reaching out into the topography of the Bible lands. The Sea of Galilee, which is a vital, living lake with fish in it and
growth around it, gets its water from Mount Hermon
above and it lets it out into the Jordan River where
it meanders south to the Dead Sea, and there it stops.
The Sea of Galilee is alive because it takes in water
from above and lets it out below. The Dead Sea *is*
dead. There is nothing living in it, and there is nothing living around it. It takes in from above, but it
does not give out below. That is the way it is with
many Christians. Many of us have received the water
of life through a long pipeline. We look back and see
that we were drawn to Christ because a host of
Christ's followers befriended us, entertained us, loved
us, and cared for us. And we have become simply a
plug in that pipeline—too busy to befriend anyone except those to whom we are indebted.

Many of us haven't stood by "the door" in a
long time. We have become so fully involved in Christian fellowship that all we hear is the familiar sounds

of our friends. The cry of the stranger has been drowned out. Be very quiet for a moment . . . can you feel the stranger's silent cry for friendship?

Ken Medema, a very talented and creative musician, has taken Matthew 25:42-45 and composed this hymn:

> I was hungry and you had no meat for
>   me;
> I was thirsty and you would not give me
>   drink.
> I was a stranger and you would not take
>   me in,
>   naked and you would not clothe me,
>   sick and you would not visit me,
>   in jail and you would not come to me,
> You would not come to me.

And then, in a fast, frivolous, defensive, exciting manner, a chorus chimes in:

> Lord, when were you hungry?
> We did not see your need.
> Lord, when were you sick, eh?
> We did not see you bleed.
> Lord, when were you in jail?
> We did not see you there.
> Were you wearin' a disguise?
> If so, it was not fair.

And the words of the Lord resound with strength:

> If you did not do it to the least of these
>   my little ones,
> then you did not do it unto me.
> I was hungry and you . . . .

The abrupt ending tosses the application right into our laps. Then the composer includes everyone in singing a kind of postscript.

> Someone is waiting right outside your
>   door.
> Someone is waiting whom you've never
>   seen before.
> Not the thousands or the millions who
>   crowd the city streets,
> But someone is lying at your feet.
> Someone is lying at your feet.[1]

Be very quiet again . . . are you aware of the stranger's silent cry for friendship. Do you care?

Notes

Chapter 2
    [1]Henri J. M. Nouwen, *Reaching Out*, (Garden City, N.Y.: Doubleday, 1975), 50.

    [2]1 John 4:20.

3   [3]Richard Collier, *The General Next to God*, (Glascow: Collins, 1965), 72.

Chapter 3
    [1]Edith Schaeffer, "Hospitality: Optional or Commanded," *Christianity Today*, December 17, 1976, 28.

    [2]*Ibid.*

    [3]*Reaching Out*, 50.

    [4]Jinx Morgan, "Heavenly Hash," *American Way*, May 1981, 123-126.

Chapter 4
    [1]James Kennedy, *Evangelism Explosion*, (Wheaton: Tyndale Publishing House, 1970).

Chapter 5
    [1]*Reaching Out*, 55.

Chapter 6
[1]Lawrence E. Moser, *Home Celebrations*, (New York: Paulist Press, 1980), 17-21.

[2]Matthew 18:20.

[3]John 8:12.

[4]Helen Smith Shoemaker, *I Stand By The Door*, (Waco: Word Books, 1967).

[5]Sunday Worship Bulletin, Mendocino Presbyterian Church, Mendocino, California, January 13, 1980.

[6]"Rite of Christian Initiation of Adults," Publishing Office of the United States Catholic Conference, Provisional Text, 1974.

Chapter 8
[1]Paul E. Little, "A Guide to International Friendship," Inter-Varsity Christian Fellowship, 1959.

[2]"Creative Entertaining," Project P.A.C.E., Community Services Division, Bureau of Alcoholism Services, County of Santa Clara, California.

Chapter 9
[1]"Stages of Grief," St. Thomas Community of Christians, Visalia, California.

Chapter 10
[1]Ken Medema, "I Was Hungry," Word Music, Inc., 1977.

Bibliography

Collier, Richard, *The General Next to God*, Collins:
Glascow, 1965.

County Services Division, Project P.A.C.E. (Prevent
Alcoholism through Community Education),
Community Services Division, Bureau of
Alcoholism Services, County of Santa Clara,
California.

Kennedy, James, *Evangelism Explosion*, Tyndale
Publishing House: Wheaton, 1970.

Little, Paul E., "A Guide to International Friendship,"
Inter-Varsity Christian Fellowship: Madison,
1959.

Mains, Karen Burton, *Open Heart, Open Home*,
David C. Cook Publishing Company: Elgin,
1976.

Medema, Ken, "I Was Hungry," Word Music, Inc.:
Waco, 1977.

Moser, Lawrence E., S.J., *Home Celebrations*, Paulist
Press: New York, 1970.

Nouwen, Henri J. M., *Reaching Out*, Doubleday &
Co., Inc.: New York, 1975.

Olford, Stephen F., D.D., "Christian Hospitality,"
Decision, Minneapolis, March 1968.

Palmer, Earl, "Ingredients of our Age," Sermon tape from First Presbyterian Church, Berkeley, California, 1974.

Revised Standard Version of the Bible, Division of Christian Education of the National Council of the Churches of Christ in the United States of America, 1952, 1946.

Ritchie, Ron, R., "Lover of Strangers," *Discovery Papers*, Peninsula Bible Church, Palo Alto, January 20, 1974.

Schaeffer, Edith, "Hospitality: Optional or Commanded," *Christianity Today*, December 17, 1976.

Shoemaker, Helen Smith, *I Stand By The Door*, Word Books: Waco, 1977.

St. Thomas Community of Christians, "Stages of Grief," Visalia, California.

Stott, John, *Christ the Liberator*, Inter-Varsity Press: Downers Grove, Illinois, 1971.

Theological Dictionary of the New Testament, Vol. V, "Biblical Basis for Hospitality," edited by G. Kittel, translated by Jeffrey W. Bromiley.

United States Catholic Conference, Publishing Office, "Rite of Christian Initiation of Adults," Washington D.C., Provisional Text, 1974.

White, Mel, *Deceived*, Spire Books, Fleming H. Revell Co.: Old Tappan, N.J., 1979.

Index

Bruce Rowlison is a graduate of the University of Minnesota, with majors in Speech and English, and of Fuller Theological Seminary. He has a Doctor of Ministry degree from the Jesuit Theological Seminary in Berkeley, California. He has been in the pastorate for over fifteen years, and is the author of *Let's Talk About Your Wedding and Marriage*.